Friends
for
Life

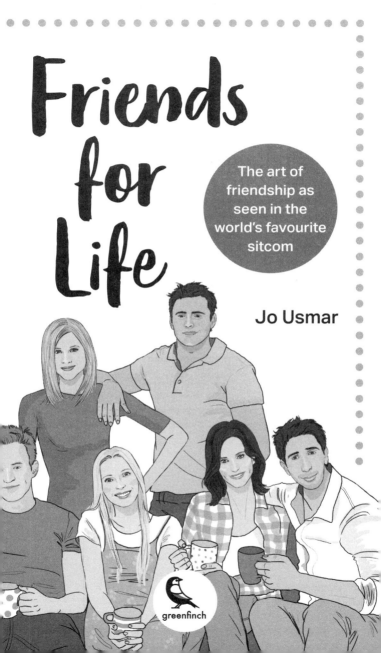

Friends for Life

The art of friendship as seen in the world's favourite sitcom

Jo Usmar

greenfinch

First published in Great Britain in 2020 by Greenfinch

An imprint of Quercus Editions Ltd
Carmelite House
50 Victoria Embankment
London EC4Y 0DZ

An Hachette UK company

A CIP catalogue record for this book is available from the British Library

HB ISBN 9781529413489

Ebook ISBN 9781529413496

10 9 8 7 6 5 4 3 2 1

Design by Tokiko Morishima

Cover and interior artwork by Mel Elliot

Printed and bound in Great Britain by Clays Ltd, Elcograf S.p.A

Papers used by Greenfinch are from well-managed forests and other responsible sources.

CONTENTS

INTRODUCTION
MAGIC BEANS

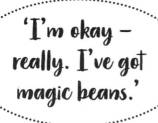

'I'm okay – really. I've got magic beans.'

Rachel, 'The One With George Stephanopoulos' (1.04)

If you haven't recently binge-watched all ten seasons of the US TV series *Friends*, firstly, you're probably feeling pretty embarrassed right now that you prioritized other things, and secondly, you might be wondering what the above quote has to do with, well, anything. While we can't fix the first issue (you should feel embarrassed – what better way is there to spend 85 hours?), the second is easily explained: it's one of the simplest and most touching descriptions of friendship from a show defined by its groundbreaking portrayal of the subject.

Rachel Green's magic beans come in the form of Monica Geller (Courteney Cox), Ross Geller (David Schwimmer), Phoebe Buffay (Lisa Kudrow), Chandler Bing (Matthew Perry) and Joey Tribbiani (Matt LeBlanc): the group of twenty- and then thirty-something New Yorkers whose close-knit exploits captivated audiences globally for ten years, from 1994 to 2004.

And yet, somehow, despite the *Friends* finale being screened more than 16 years ago (and reaching 52.5 million viewers in America alone), this group of disparate characters continues to beguile both returning fans and new devotees alike.

Consistently ranked as one of the most-watched shows on Netflix since the streaming platform bought the rights from Warner Bros in 2015, Marta Kauffman and David Crane's sitcom still resonates with viewers of all ages. But why? What is it about this show in particular that inspires such devotion? As Saul Austerlitz writes in his book *Still Friends: 25 Years of the TV Show that Defined an Era*, it is impossible not to wonder at 'the remarkable life and afterlife of this show, which still captivates new audiences a quarter of a century later.'*

The answer is all in the magic beans.

---

* Saul Austerlitz: *Still Friends: 25 Years of the TV Show that Defined an Era* (Trapeze, 2019)

SO, NO ONE TOLD YOU LIFE WAS GONNA BE THIS WAY

The magic is sewn from the very first episode, when Rachel (Jennifer Aniston) bursts into a New York coffee spot in a soaking-wet wedding dress, having left her fiancé, orthodontist Barry, at the altar.

She is quickly folded into her old school friend Monica's group, offered a place to stay and reassured that having no money, no job and absolutely no idea what to do with her life is perfectly acceptable. (Four episodes in, when asked if she has a life plan, Phoebe sighs: 'I don't even have a pl...')

In this first season we learn that Phoebe's mum died by suicide, Joey's father is cheating on his mother, Chandler's father and mother both had (separate) affairs with the pool boy, Ross's ex-wife Carol (Jane Sibbett) left him for a woman and is pregnant with his baby, and Monica's parents constantly put her down. In comparison to everyone else's problems, Rachel ditching her ready-made suburban life seems relatively small fry.

And that's the allure of the show. Sudden catastrophic life events and slow-burn traumas aren't ignored in favour of surface-level LOLs, but are addressed in relatable, comforting and funny ways. Things like divorce, unrequited love, break-ups, unemployment, infertility, money issues, problematic families, sexual indiscretions and insecurities, mental health and loneliness are tackled by a group of friends who, just like you, also spend hours on the couch staring into space, or debating their life decisions over a posh coffee they can't really afford.

THE ONE WITH THE ISSUES

***Friends* didn't always get it right** and much has been written recently about how certain aspects haven't aged well. There's the fact the primary cast is all white and middle-class, the LGBTQ characters aren't well-rounded, homosexuality is often played for laughs, 'Fat Monica' is body-shamed and Ross's behaviour can be controlling. One of the most discussed issues is the treatment of Chandler's transgender father, Helena, who is always referred to as 'he' and described as either a gay man or drag queen, never trans.

Yet, *Friends* has to be judged within the context of the time it was made. The fact there was a trans character at all on a middle-of-the-road sitcom was pretty progressive. Kathleen Turner, who played Helena, has since explained, 'I said yes [to the role], because there weren't many drag/trans people on television at the time.'* And then there's the conflict between the 'being seen as gay' panic the male characters exhibit and the fact the show was one of the first on US TV to feature a gay wedding – one officiated by LGBTQ activist Candace Gingrich no less, half-sister to conservative Republican Newt Gingrich. (It's also worth noting that show co-creator David Crane is himself gay.) And, while there are few substantial roles for actors of colour on the show, the interracial relationships are portrayed straightforwardly and unaffectedly.

Friends was also one of the first sitcoms to offer equal billing to both male and female stars with the characters of Monica, Rachel and Phoebe not merely foils for the 'main' male roles.

---

* http://www.gaytimes.co.uk/culture/friends-actress-kathleen-turner-says-show-hasnt-aged-well-lgbtq-rights-exclusive/, accessed 17 Aug. 2020.

Even the fact the women unapologetically engage in one-night stands and endure no great emotional or societal repercussions was, depressingly enough, revelatory for a Thursday evening prime-time comedy show – as was their casual discussions about sex and female sexual pleasure (perfectly encapsulated by Monica's lesson to Chandler on erogenous zones in 'The One With Phoebe's Uterus' (4.11)).

The cast also famously stuck together in insisting on equal pay in later seasons after Aniston's and Schwimmer's salaries were increased due to the popularity of their relationship storyline. (Aniston and Schwimmer agreed to pay cuts so everyone would earn the same.)

So, while there's no denying there are problems with *Friends'* handling of sensitive cultural subjects, at least it didn't ignore them altogether, as many other shows did at the time. In addressing them at all, it pushed the envelope of what was considered 'expected' on television and, as Austerlitz says, 'In its embrace of the aggressively normal in its storytelling, it was able to expand the spectrum of normalcy until it could also include a lesbian wedding.'

To disregard these discussions around the oftentimes flawed way the show tackled certain issues would be to undermine its cultural importance. The fact they're talked about with such passion proves the continuing impact of a series that people still care deeply about.

THE ONE WHERE YOU MAKE FRIENDS FOR LIFE

Matt LeBlanc told the BBC in 2018: '*Friends* was about themes that stand the test of time – trust, love, relationships, betrayal, family and things like that.'* These themes have never been so relevant than they are right now in this post-Covid world. When the rug is pulled from under you, priorities are reassessed and focus inevitably turns to companionship.

Perhaps that's why the show is enjoying such a revival, because it taps into our desire to have the safety and comfort of a group of ride-or-die friends. It also delivers the nostalgia of what can now be seen as a simpler time – no smartphones, no online dating, no 24/7 work culture (the characters are barely ever at work, to be fair), no social media…and no Covid-19. Or perhaps it's because it's always reassuring to see other people decidedly *not* holding their shit together when the pressure to present a perfect life on Instagram or be hilarious on TikTok is all too real.

At its heart the show is a love story about friendship, with all its highs and lows. Having magic beans means that when life kicks you in the teeth (especially if they're luminous like Ross's in 'The One With Ross's Teeth' (6.08)), you know you'll come out stronger on the other side. And what's better than that? Nothing! Which is why we created this book – to investigate the biggest, best and funniest lessons in friendship from the series. Whether it's knowing when to apologize, administer

---

* https://www.bbc.co.uk/news/entertainment-arts-42733705, accessed 17 Aug. 2020.

some tough love, phase someone out, be supportive (even if you really don't want to be), discuss money problems or to scream about how you definitely were on a break, this book will help ensure you'll make *Friends for Life*.

Reserved for Friends

If you've ever wondered why the big comfy couch in the coffee shop is always available, it's actually reserved for the gang. A sign on the coffee table is visible in several episodes. The only two times it's occupied by other people are made into comedy moments. In 'The One With the Bullies' (2.21), Chandler and Ross are forced off the couch and in 'The One With the Princess Leia Fantasy' (3.01), the group reverse out the door in shock upon finding it occupied by other people.

WHAT KIND OF 'FRIEND' ARE YOU?

Answer the below questions and add up your points to find out on pages 16–17.

When I disagree with my friend...

20 – I often have a knee-jerk emotional reaction
0 – I explain my point of view in detail
10 – I make a few jokes about the issue, but don't push it

When they're going through a hard time...

10 – I'll provide drinks, ice cream, jokes and hugs
20 – I'll invent a best-case scenario fantasy to make them feel better
0 – I'll make a plan for the best way to tackle the problem

When playing a game with a group of mates...

0 – I'll pretend I'm having fun, but really I need to win
10 – I'll try my best, but it won't bother me if someone else wins
20 – I forgot the rules immediately so now am just playing a made-up game in my head

When I have to tell my friend bad news...

10 – I avoid it and hope someone else does it
0 – I tell them immediately, no point hanging about
20 – I'll tell them when it's a good time (and I can comfort them with cookies)

If I don't like my friend's new partner...

20 – I'll give them the benefit of the doubt until there's no getting around it
10 – I'll avoid them and make awkward jokes behind their backs for a while
0 – I'm too wrapped up in my own life right now to notice to be honest

When my friend asks me to help move a couch up three flights of stairs...

0 – Sure thing. It might be entertaining and it's part and parcel of being a good mate
20 – I'll say, 'I wish I could, but I don't want to'
10 – I'll go, but will moan about it the whole time

RESULTS

0–20 points: ROSS

Logical and detail-oriented, you'll offer friends advice and encouragement based upon what you see as the reality of the situation. While practical, this means you occasionally underestimate the emotional side of issues and have a tendency to project your own views rather forcefully. However, upon realizing this you'll be sure to do your best to hear their side.

30–40 points: MONICA

Organized and driven, everything has its correct place – including your mates. A people-pleaser, you're the glue that holds the group together, enthusiastically supporting, comforting and feeding everyone. Your belief in how things should be done makes you a bit bossy and a bit too fact driven, but you're self-aware enough to know that sometimes offering a hug is better than making a plan.

50–60 points: CHANDLER

Intuitive, you'll know when something's up with your friends and want to help despite not being sure what to do. You use humour both as a defence mechanism and to keep your friends humble, always pointing out the elephant in the room. You'll want to keep the peace, but not at the expense of someone's feelings – you're more sensitive than you make out.

70–80 points: RACHEL

Emotionally driven, you'll put your friends' needs first without hesitation. Not a fan of either receiving or delivering tough love, you'll avoid uncomfortable situations even if it makes life harder in the long run. Laid-back, you're happy to go along with plans which means your mates may occasionally take advantage of your easy-going nature.

90–100 points: JOEY

Loud and fun, the entertainer of the group, you're also super-sensitive, listening to your heart more than your head on occasion. This means you not only give a lot to your friends, but demand a lot in return. Loyal to a fault, you'll stand up for your friends…often before knowing the full story.

100–120 points: PHOEBE

Inherently self-confident, you accept your friends wholeheartedly just as they are. You don't take offence where others might, which can sometimes mean underestimating the effect of your own blunt honesty. You call things as you see them while always supporting your friends' dreams and aspirations (the more outlandish the better).

CHAPTER 1
THE ONE WHERE FRIENDS BECOME FAMILY

> '**Boyfriends and girlfriends are gonna come and go, but this is for life.**'

Phoebe, 'The One With All the Cheesecakes' (7.11)

When Marta Kauffman and David Crane pitched a show called *Insomnia Cafe* to NBC in 1993, about a group of twenty-somethings hanging out in a coffee shop, the tagline was: 'It's that time of life when your friends are your family.'*

They were right. Societal and cultural norms were being redefined in the 1990s, in both the UK and US. Generation X (those born between 1965 and 1980) were emerging, battered and bruised, from a decade remembered for a global recession and record divorce rates. The systems that had defined life for their boomer parents were exposed as riddled with cracks. Securing a job for life and settling down were no longer necessarily feasible or desirable goals for a disaffected youth. They wanted to chase creative, more fulfilling paths – or bitch about their dead-end jobs and non-existent aspirations with people in the same leaky boat: their friends.

*Saul Austerlitz: *Still Friends: 25 Years of a TV Show That Defined An Era*

It was an era when this Harper Lee line came into its own: 'You can choose your friends, but you sho' can't choose your family'.

Many TV networks recognized this cultural shift and set out to discover the next *Seinfeld*, which was groundbreaking in its focus on a friendship- rather than family-group dynamic. Young people wanted to watch shows that reflected their own realities, or the realities they dreamed of: starting somewhere new with people who 'get' them. *Friends* met that need, portraying six relatively clueless pals, all searching for more from life…while terrified, at the same time, that they might actually get it.

THE NEW NORMAL

The show established its Gen X credentials from the off. In the pilot episode, viewers meet Ross, who's just been left by his wife, and then Rachel, who's sprinted from her own wedding having realized she was more turned on by a gravy boat than her husband-to-be. The episode ends with the group ceremoniously cutting up Rachel's credit cards (which are paid for by her father), thus completing the symbolic severing of ties to traditional domestic structures.

MONICA:
Welcome to the real world. It sucks. You're going to love it!

It's true that traditionalism does win out in the end: Rachel gives up her dream job in Paris to stay with Ross; Monica and Chandler move to the suburbs to raise their kids; and Phoebe, the least 'conventional' of the crew, gets married. It's only Joey who stays resolutely the same: single in the city (however, that in itself could be seen as a fulfilment of his stereotypical role of eternal bachelor).

However, the series consistently portrays the internal conflict these decisions provoke – between playing it safe versus being brave, caring what others think versus not caring at all and doing what you think you should do, rather than what you actually want to do. Examples include Phoebe taking a job at a corporate spa chain despite it conflicting with her anti-capitalist values (9.21); Chandler accepting a promotion for the money while hating his job (1.15); the guys forcing themselves to 'party like Gandalf' even though they'd much rather be watching TV in their pants (4.09); and Rachel running in the park like a kid, inspired by Phoebe, even though it doesn't look cool (6.07).

This struggle is so timeless, and so expertly navigated in the show, it is undoubtedly one of the key reasons *Friends* strikes a chord with new millennial viewers. We're all guilty of posting a snap of ourselves having an 'amazing' time at a party, when in reality it sucked. And we've all wondered 'Should I be doing that?' when someone reveals they've ditched their job to run a surf school in Thailand. So, it's entirely reassuring to realize that 25 years ago, pre-social media, the gang of 6 were experiencing these exact same worries.

And the reason all of this matters – both then and now – is that while you may struggle being honest with your family, or even with strangers on social media, you can tell the truth to your friends. So even though Aunt Sarah thinks you really should be married by now and Philanthropic Phil on Facebook reckons you're a sell-out, it doesn't matter, because your pals know what's actually going on and they've got your back, no matter what.

YOUR FRIENDS HELP YOU DEAL WITH YOUR 'REAL' FAMILY

True friends allow you the space to forge a personality and path for yourself, one not dictated by selfish needs, obligation or societal expectation. Rachel's journey of self-discovery, enabled by the support she garners from her 'magic beans', is the framework upon which the first season – and arguably the entire show – is built. She's not only fighting against her parents' expectations and their belief she can't manage alone, but her own secret fear that they might be right.

Because of this, when her mother reveals she's considering leaving Rachel's father after being inspired by her daughter's bravery – 'You didn't marry your Barry, honey, but I married mine.' (2.11) – it's a real moment of emotional catharsis for both Rachel and viewers. As is the revelation from her sister Jill in Season 6 that, in spite of his terrifying demeanour, her father is proud of her. Viewers share the pride and relief she feels that her decision to lean on her friends, trust her instincts and take risks has not only paid off, but is recognized by those she left behind.

Truth is, most of us spend much more time with our friends than our family, be it in person or via WhatsApp. It's our friends who see us at our best, worst, strongest and weakest. They pick us up when we're down, revel in our successes, commiserate with our failures and dish out tough love when necessary. They hold a mirror up to our behaviour – which is particularly important when it comes to our relatives.

All the parental and sibling relationships depicted on the show are complicated (including Ross and Monica's). There's Judy's never-ending criticism of Monica, Rachel's fear of her controlling and narcissistic dad, Joey's father-like role to his many sisters, Chandler's trauma over his mum and dad's divorce – and where to even start with Phoebe?

The show doesn't shy away from addressing the trauma and scars of childhood, and does so in a matter-of-fact and hilarious way, which was, and remains, unique. *Friends* normalizes the fact that everyone's a product of their messed-up past and then mitigates the horror by showing us it will be okay because our friends will step up.

When Phoebe changes Judy's awful 'pulled a Monica' phrase into a positive rather than a negative, when Ross encourages Chandler to confront his mum about the fact she kissed him, and when Joey and Chandler and then Joey and Rachel

Rachel Karen Green

NICKNAMES/ALIASES: Rach; Green; Ray-Ray; Racquel; Mrs Geller.

PARENTS: Leonard and Sandra Green.

SIBLINGS: Jill and Amy Green.

RELATIONSHIPS: Chip; Barry (fiancé who she leaves at the altar); Paolo; Russ (Ross lookalike); Joshua; Paul; Tag; Gavin; Joey; Ross.

CHILDREN: Emma Geller-Green (father: Ross).

HISTORY WITH THE FRIENDS: Known Monica Geller (and therefore also Ross) since they were kids, but they lost touch after high school. They reconnect and Rachel meets the rest of the gang when Monica lets her move in after she leaves Barry at the altar. (An inconsistency within the show can be noted around her past with Chandler. She meets him when he's with Ross several times during flashback episodes – she even snogs him at a college party (10.11) – however, in 1.01 they introduce themselves to each other as if they've never met before.)

CHILDHOOD: Spoiled upbringing with rich, unhappy parents. Very popular at school, unlike best friend Monica, but she was a bit of a mean girl (she bullied Will (Brad Pitt) who ended up founding the 'I Hate Rachel Green Club' with Ross and a foreign exchange student). Also famously had plastic surgery on her nose.

PROFESSION: Terrible waitress; assistant at Fortunata Fashions; assistant buyer and personal shopper at Bloomingdale's; executive at Ralph Lauren; accepts a position at Louis Vuitton in Paris (but in finale decides to stay in New York to be with Ross).

KEY FLASHBACK MOMENT: Chandler, overhearing Rachel tell her sorority friends she is keen for one last fling before marrying Barry, tries to get her attention (3.06). She ignores him…but fantasizes about him later on. (This ties into the conflict over when they first met – as they actually should have known each other at this point.)

PERSONALITY: Playful, funny, enthusiastic, brave, flexible, driven, laid-back and spoiled. An extrovert, while she can be a pushover about some things, she fights for what she cares about (i.e. standing up to Gavin at work after returning from maternity leave (9.11)). She really doesn't like arguments among her friends so often finds herself in the role of peace-maker, however, she's emotionally driven so can't hide her feelings.

MEMORABLE QUOTE: 'Isn't that just kick-you-in-the-crotch-spit-on-your-neck fantastic?'

INTERESTING FACT: Most commonly spelled 'Green' (this is the spelling on the end credits for her 'parents'), Rachel's surname can be seen spelled as 'Greene' several times, most obviously in 'The One With the Invitation' (4.21), when she looks at Ross and Emily's wedding invite.

separately go with Phoebe to sit in her cab outside her dad's house, it's empowering. Friends can give you an objective view on emotionally charged situations, steering you into healthier ways of dealing with them.

We can get stuck in a rut within our families – stuck in the roles we were assigned as children or that we manufactured ourselves as a coping mechanism (i.e. the overachiever, the disappointment, the joker, the carer, the black sheep). It's our friends who convince us that those roles don't have to define us indefinitely.

EXPERIENCING FIRSTS TOGETHER

Experiencing firsts together – things that would usually take place in childhood, be typically taught by a family member, involve parental guidance or be a relative's 'job' to undertake – can bond friends for life. The series documents these moments beautifully:

- **Ross teaches Phoebe to ride a bike. (7.09)**
- **Ross helps Rachel to do her own laundry. (1.05)**

- Rachel is with Ross when Ben, his son, says his first word. (2.20)
- Phoebe helps Chandler to break up with Janice – his first break-up that doesn't involve awkwardly handing whoever it is a note. (1.05)
- The gang's all there to celebrate and then commiserate when Rachel receives her first waitressing pay cheque: 'Who's FICA? Why's he getting all my money?' (1.04)
- Chandler teaches Joey how to pay the bills. (6.06)
- Chandler walks Phoebe down the aisle. (10.12)

These examples demonstrate how defining friendship moments are often found in everyday activities. They become extraordinary because your friends have understood your need, stepped up and been there for you. In lieu of relatives, friends can be there to support you in all the life lessons you never realized you needed to learn.

The Joy of Doing Nothing Together

One of the true tests of friendship is when you're comfortable doing absolutely sod-all together. Some of the best, most reassuring, scenes in the show are when they're all bundled on the couch watching TV. It's this mundanity that denotes comfortableness. When you don't have to talk all the time, or entertain each other. Indeed, one of the funniest, and weirdly most appealing, story arcs is when Joey, flush from his first stint on *Days of our Lives*, buys himself and Chandler big leather BarcaLoungers (2.15). 'Sweet mother of all that is good and pure', Chandler gasps upon seeing them. They don't leave the chairs for days.

This slovenly companionship speaks to a security that comes from knowing neither of you would rather be doing anything else. Nowadays, viewers will watch this and wonder at the simplicity and peace of no one checking their phone every two minutes or being distracted by pinging notifications. It's just you, your friends and *Baywatch*. A simpler time.

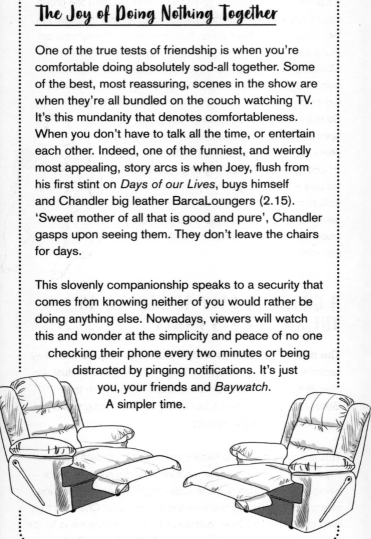

It's perhaps unsurprising, given this closeness, that the group spend most 'family' holidays together, a tradition that starts in Season 1 with Thanksgiving. After everyone's family-oriented plans backfire, the group end up eating grilled cheese in Monica and Rachel's apartment. When Joey says 'This was nobody's first choice' (1.09), the writers knew most viewers would be thinking how it actually looked pretty great.

So much so that the fact they then go on to spend Thanksgiving together for the next nine years makes total sense. And indeed 'Friendsgiving' – a Thanksgiving meal just for pals – is now a genuine part of holiday culture in the States. And why not? It makes sense to celebrate with friends if they're the ones who provide a sense of family year-round.

A GROUP IS ONLY AS STRONG AS THE SUM OF ITS PARTS

The micro-friendships within the larger squad are a key factor in the group's longevity. They not only serve to illustrate how deep and complex different relationships (with their different histories) can be, but also give a rare insight into the joy of co-ed friendship groups.

This is a real part of the show's charm. Messing with gender expectations in softly-softly ways was the show's reason for being. Sure, the men play the easy-laugh lechery card far too often, but then there's the time the women take Chandler to a strip club after he's been dumped (4.14); how Phoebe is by far the most sexually adventurous; how Rachel dumps Paul

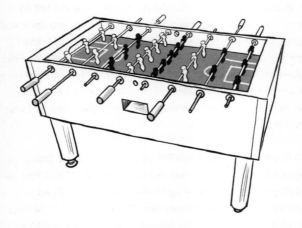

Stevens (Bruce Willis in one of the best cameos ever) for being too emotional (6.23); how Monica is the best foosball player; and how proud Chandler is that he can expertly pluck Joey's eyebrows (9.13). The best example though, of course, is when Chandler and Joey win Monica and Rachel's apartment because they know them better (4.12). Following gender stereotypes typical of this era, the women, as classic nurturers, would be expected to better remember the minutiae of the men's lives. That they don't, and that the men are then rewarded for their win by taking the women's home, is a very funny way of rubbishing gender norms.

Sure there's flirting between everyone within the group and 'what if?' hook-up scenarios are investigated in flashback episodes, but it is the underlying constant of the platonic friendships they all share that is at the heart of the show. The friendships are just that: friendships. Indeed, viewers felt so strongly about this that the backlash triggered by the Joey and Rachel storyline in Season 10 was swift and brutal. People liked the simplicity and joy of the uncomplicated and authentic male–female friendships that didn't cross the line into romance (an accidental snog notwithstanding). It reassured everyone that adult men and women could be 'just friends' and that was better than anything else.

This is why it's so great that Phoebe and Joey have dinner once a month 'to discuss the rest of you guys' (7.11); Chandler and Rachel regularly meet up at their respective offices for lunch, or to eat stolen cheesecake off the floor (7.11); Monica uncomplainingly feeds Joey everyday; and Monica and Ross share a (sometimes disconcertingly) close sibling relationship (anyone else still traumatized by the pile-of-coats kissing incident recounted in Season 10?).

Top Five Cameos

These five cameos were all nominated for the Outstanding Guest Actor/Actress in a Comedy Series Emmy Awards, with Bruce Willis and Christina Applegate scooping trophies in 2000 and 2003 respectively.

1. Bruce Willis

Willis only appeared as Paul Stevens, the overprotective father of Ross's much younger girlfriend Elizabeth, after losing a bet to Matthew Perry on the set of *The Whole Nine Yards*. His three-episode stint in Season 6 saw him intimidate and belittle Ross, date Rachel, psych himself up in the mirror ('You're just a love machine!') and weep uncontrollably after Rachel convinces him to be more emotional.

2. Christina Applegate

Christina Applegate's Amy Green appears in 'The One With Rachel's Other Sister' (9.08) and 'The One Where Rachel's Sister Babysits' (10.05). Her inability to remember her niece Emma's name and her belief that Ross is the falafel guy are iconic (Joey: 'She may be the hottest girl I've ever hated').

3. Gary Oldman

Oldman played Richard Crosby, Joey's spitting World War 1 film co-star in Season 7. His on-set drunkenness nearly causes Joey to miss Chandler and Monica's wedding.

4. Susan Sarandon

Sarandon plays *Days of our Lives* star Cecilia Monroe, who discovers Dr Drake Ramoray is going to receive her dead character's brain in a pioneering transplant operation. It's one of the few genuinely heartfelt romantic storylines for Joey.

5. Brad Pitt

Probably the most famous cameo (though arguably not the funniest), Pitt is newly hot Will, Monica and Ross's old school friend, who co-founded the 'I Hate Rachel Green Club' with Ross while they were teenagers (8.09).

Special mentions: Jennifer Coolidge, Winona Ryder, Danny DeVito, Jon Lovitz, Julia Roberts, and Billy Crystal and Robin Williams.

The definition of a cameo:
a guest appearance by a well-known name for a maximum of three episodes that covers a one-off storyline. (So Tom Selleck as Richard doesn't qualify as he's a secondary character, appearing in ten episodes across several seasons. Same goes for Paul Rudd as Mike.)

And then, of course, there's Joey and Chandler. Not a co-ed friendship, but the most successful one on the show. Just like Laurel and Hardy, who adorn a big poster on their wall, Joey and Chandler's bromance sets the bar for heterosexual male friendship, constantly veering into coupledom.

Their relationship forms the basis for many of the most meaningful friendship lessons: betrayal, lying, apologizing, lending money, living together, moving out, asking for help and also jealousy. They epitomize the ethos of the show: that friendship should always be the priority, be it over romance or work commitments. In Season 8, now Monica and Chandler are married, Joey tells Chandler that he misses him and they promise to make more time for each other. Close bonds like this demand work and should never be taken for granted. The same happens within the female group when Rachel gets jealous of the time Monica is spending with Julie, Ross's new girlfriend: 'Just because I'm friends with her, doesn't make me any less friends with you', Monica reassures her (2.02).

Friendship is a two-way street. You expect things from your friends, just as they expect things from you. There's a natural ebb and flow, but because you have chosen these people, you have to earn them – you have to put the work in – because unlike family, there's no obligation for friends to be around for ever. This makes the bond special. You put in the work because the rewards are so worth it.

LESSONS LEARNED

- Friends can step up when family falls short.

- We tend to spend more time with friends than family, so they see us at our best and worst. That gives these relationships an honesty that should be treasured.

- You choose your friends (unlike family) so these relationships demand time and energy. Put the work in and you'll reap the rewards.

CHAPTER 2
THE ONE WITH
THE PHASE-OUT, CUT-OUT
OR FRENAISSANCE

> 'It was just a matter of time before someone had to leave the group. I just always assumed Phoebe would be the one to go.'

Rachel, 'The One With the Kips' (5.05)

According to the show, there are two ways to ditch your friends:

- **THE PHASE-OUT:** a gradual drifting apart (either deliberate or undeliberate).
- **THE CUT-OUT:** a very deliberate severing of ties because you've decided your life would be better without them in it.

In 'The One With All the Kips' (5.05), Rachel discovers Ross has agreed to Emily's demand that he not see her anymore. Despite everyone else's assurances that this won't affect her relationship with them, Rachel is sure she's about to suffer the same fate as 'Kip'. Poor old Kip was Chandler's ex-roommate and Monica's ex-fling. When he and Monica ended things, even though everyone liked him, he got phased out due to the awkwardness with Monica: he was invited to less and less events and people stopped returning his messages. Uncalculated, this instance was solely caused by circumstance, however, phase-outs can be deliberate, distancing yourself due to changes in behaviour or in your feelings towards someone. Phase-outs aren't always the death knell for friendship, sometimes they can give you space to work out what's going on and what you want to do about it. (Phoebe's an expert at this, employing it on pretty much all the friends at some point).

Meanwhile, in 'The One With Ross's Tan' (10.03), Monica and Phoebe's ex-neighbour, Amanda Buffamonteezi (Jennifer Coolidge in a gleeful cameo), rocks back into town with an outrageous British accent and a great line in bizarre self-aggrandizement ('Smell my neck! It's not perfume, it's me. It's my natural scent!'). Phoebe suggests they cut her out: 'Just ignore her calls and dodge her till she gets the point'. Despite Monica describing this as harsh and Chandler admitting he's been on the receiving end of it once and it 'feels good!' (sarcastic), they push ahead with the plan.

Now, for every negative action there's a positive reaction and in this context that comes in the form of a 'frenaissance'. Introduced as a concept in 'The One After Vegas' (6.01) by Phoebe when Joey sells their road trip home as a chance to reconnect, a frenaissance is a renewal or rebirth of a waning or neglected friendship. (Phoebe agrees to the idea, but says 'Although I don't think we really need one baby, I never stopped loving you.')

Here's how to know whether it's time for a phase-out, cut-out or frenaissance with your own friends.

WHY YOU MIGHT NEED TO PHASE OUT OR CUT OUT

In simple terms: because people change, circumstances change and friendships change. Why are you still hanging out with your old school friend Lucy if you have nothing to say to each other? Why are you still calling James if you can't stand him? Even newish friends can grow apart, have an unfixable argument or move to Minsk. Any of these things warrant a relationship reassessment. Friends are people we *choose* to stay in touch with (unlike family who you're kind of stuck with), so you need to ask yourself why you're wasting precious time on someone that makes you feel 'meh' or worse. Life's too short. As a way of separating the friend-wheat from the chaff, try categorizing your pals into either 'radiators' or 'drains':

- **DRAINS: people who drain you of energy, motivation or confidence. The kind of folk that suck away all of your enthusiasm like LOL vampires, leaving you feeling negative, cranky, defensive, deflated and insecure.**

- **RADIATORS: people who lift you up, support you and make you smile. They're buzzy, fun and their positivity is contagious. They're interested and interesting.**

A good way to work out if your friends fit into these categories is to assess your feelings when you're on the way to meet them. Are you: upbeat, enthusiastic and excited; or wary, defensive and resigned? Also, check into your physical response: do they leave you standing tall with a big smile, or hunched over and exhausted? You may have got so used to physically psyching yourself up to meet Debbie Downer that you don't even notice your clenched fists and fake smile anymore.

A quick analysis of some secondary characters on the show:

- **DRAINS:** Fun Bobby when he stops drinking (very problematic, we know); Rachel's entire family except her mum; Mr Heckles; Gunther (sorry, but true); Monica and Ross's mum, Judy; Susan.
- **RADIATORS:** Gandalf (we never met him, but jeez, that guy lights up a room); Monica and Ross's dad, Jack; Janice (we'll fight you on this); Richard; Julie; Kathy.

Not everyone will either be a drain or a radiator – people have complex and varied personalities and we're friends with them for complex and varied reasons. The quiz on pages 44–45 will therefore help too, getting you to step back and view the friendship objectively by asking some simple questions. Is your friendship balanced? Do they have your best interests at heart? Are you friends because you actually like each other or only because you always have been? Do you want to put more effort in or aren't you bothered? Tapping into your emotional and physical reactions to people and assessing the reality of your relationship from an outsider's perspective can be very revealing.

SO, WHAT'S THE PLAN? PHASE OUT, CUT OUT OR FRENAISSANCE?

WARNING: Both phasing out and cutting out will cause confusion and hurt if you don't address why you're doing it with the person on the receiving end (and yes, they will notice it's happening). Put yourself in their shoes: wouldn't you want an explanation rather than filling in the blanks yourself?

Phase Out

Depending on how close you are with the person you're planning on phasing out, backing off from a friendship can be incredibly distressing to the other party if it comes out of the blue. We sincerely hope the group explained to Kip why they weren't inviting him to stuff anymore, but judging by their inability to deal with anything straightforwardly, we doubt it. Also, make sure *you* know why you're doing it. Is it the result of a knee-jerk reaction to something they've said or done and, rather than address it, you're taking the 'easy' way out by distancing yourself?

The healthiest phase-out is when you tell people you need a break and explain why — maybe because of their controlling nature (Phoebe to Monica) or their jealousy (Rachel to Ross). Getting some space can be necessary to work out how you really feel about the relationship: do you feel better now you're less available to them or do you miss them a lot? And then assess what that says about your friendship: are you willing to discuss the problems and fight for it, continue as mates but on a different footing (i.e. less close), or do you want to let it go altogether?

Cut Out

Okay, so let's get something straight from the off: CUTTING PEOPLE OUT WITHOUT ANY EXPLANATION IS AWFUL. Didn't you hear the trauma dripping from Chandler's sarcastic 'Feels good!' when talking about how he'd once been cut out? The equivalent nowadays is, of course, ghosting. Social media is the great enabler of this cowardly and mean way of eliminating someone from your life. Being able to leave someone 'on read' (where they can see you've read their message but you haven't responded) is a brutal but easy way of not dealing with a situation. Who would have guessed back in the 1990s that so much of the new millennium's anxiety problems would be caused by two little blue ticks?

Anyone who has ever been ghosted knows the anxiety, self-doubt and genuine pain that comes from being ignored and not knowing why. This is an unacceptable way to behave. I don't care how awful (for 'awful' read 'brilliant') Amanda Buffamonteezi is — she doesn't deserve to be ghosted. No one does (unless they're physically or emotionally abusive, and then ghost away, quick-smart (see pages 44–45)). If either Monica or Phoebe had spoken to Amanda about her mad and rude behaviour, perhaps she would have reined it in. At least she would have had the option to try. The worst thing about Phoebe's encouragement to use the tactic is that she knows it's rubbish, admitting how she once tried to cut Monica out but Monica had fought her way back and now Phoebe admits, 'I don't know what I'd do without you'.

Phoebe owed Monica a conversation, like the one they had when she finally admitted she'd moved out (3.06). Sure, it was awkward and unpleasant, but it saved their friendship. And, if you're prepared to lose them anyway by cutting them out, isn't it worth giving them one last shot at making things right? They may surprise you with explanations for their behaviour if they've hurt you, they may up their game or may agree that things have run their course. Whatever the response, you owe a friend the truth so they're not left wondering what went wrong.

Frenaissance

If you decide your friend is worth fighting for or if you've simply drifted apart due to circumstances outside of your control, it's time to reignite the friendship with a frenaissance. This means making a conscious effort to up your friend game: putting time aside for them, putting in dates to see each other and *not* cancelling (even if sex is on the cards – see Chapter 3), messaging more frequently and ensuring the relationship is balanced and that you're paying attention to them and their needs. The best thing about a frenaissance is that you don't need to wait until a friendship needs it; everyone loves to feel loved, so showering your friend with a bit more attention is never a bad thing. Also, don't always wait for someone else to make the frenaissance first move. We can often feel neglected when we feel low, when in reality our pal is just busy or distracted. Don't read into things that aren't true, be the bigger person and make an effort to show your friend that they're in your thoughts. Channel your inner Joey and Phoebe and you'll be fine.

LESSONS LEARNED

- Phase outs can help you to get a better perspective on a relationship. However, you should still explain to your friend why you need some distance.

- Cut outs are only acceptable if you explain your reasoning to the person you're about to ghost. It's the right thing to do and also gives them a chance to up their game.

- A frenaissance is a beautiful thing. Make the first move: call them, organize to see them, and like their social media posts. Make them feel loved and you'll feel loved in return.

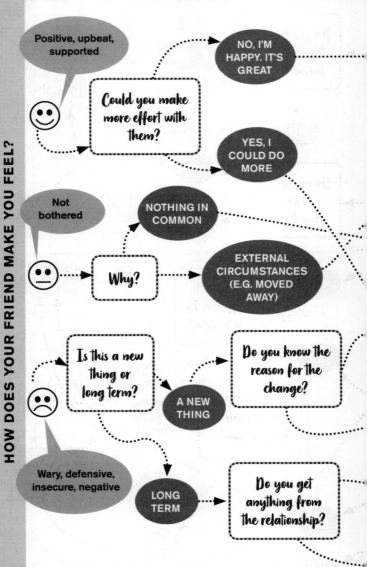

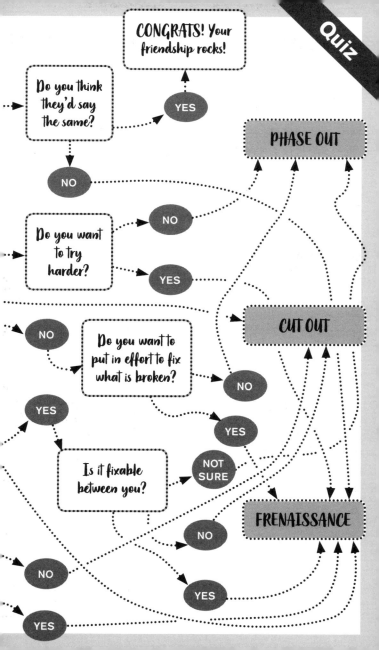

CHAPTER 3
THE ONE WHERE YOU LIVE TOGETHER

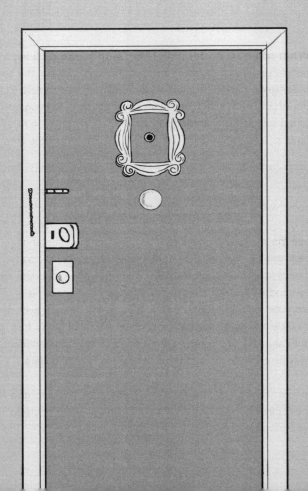

'And I have to live with a boy!'

Monica, 'The One on the Last Night' (6.06)

What could be better than living with friends? Surely the people you choose to share most of your time with are the best possible candidates to share a home with, right? NO. ARE YOU INSANE? Living with friends can either be the best thing ever or a disaster on the scale of *Armageddon* (the film). The middle ground – where you all enjoy it about 80 per cent of the time – is the sweet spot everyone should aim for.

Friends gives an entirely skewed perception of the reality of cohabitation. (For simplicity's sake, for the remainder of this book the 'women's apartment' will be referred to as 'Monica's' and the 'men's apartment' as 'Joey's' as the longest-standing residents.) First of all, it's actually more of a commune than a typical apartment-share. Neither Joey's nor Monica's doors are ever locked (indeed, the few occasions they are become storyline fodder), people come and go as they please, everyone considers Monica's kitchen an all-you-can-eat buffet (a free one) and because none of them have any other 'proper' friends, they bypass issues regarding unwanted parties or guests.

In reality these things would be unsustainable and unforgivable, inevitably leading to a fracturing of any friendship. For starters: who pays for all the food that everyone eats at Monica's? This is mentioned occasionally in passing terms as the cost of feeding Joey, but in real life that cost and presumption would be a deal-breaker — as would the annoyance of having to shop for six people rather than two and never knowing who'll be in when you get home. However, the show does confront other issues regarding living together head-on, and even the omissions teach us what we personally could and couldn't put up with (Joey: buy your own food).

Here are the best friend-cohabitation rules we learned over the ten seasons.

GOOD FRIENDS DON'T AUTOMATICALLY MAKE GOOD ROOMMATES

The series addresses a fundamental truth early on: just because you love each other as friends doesn't mean you'll love each other as roommates. In 'The One With the Flashback' (3.06), Phoebe has been living with her grandmother for a week and still hasn't told Monica that she's moved out of their shared apartment. Instead, she quietly removes all of her things, sneaks in in the morning and sneaks out after dark. She doesn't want to address *why* she's had to move out as she knows it will hurt Monica's feelings, but in avoiding the subject she makes both of their lives more difficult — and hurts Monica more.

The truth is: Monica is anal and passively-aggressively brings up things Phoebe does that annoy her, rather than addressing them directly. For example: saying she's sorry for getting lipstick on the phone when she knows it was actually Phoebe, moving things Phoebe has put down back to their correct place and

generally needing everything spotlessly clean, regimented and under control.

When Phoebe does finally confront the issue, explaining how she couldn't sleep for a month knowing she'd got an ink spot on one of the cushions, Monica is indeed hurt, but, realizing this is a deal-breaker, tries to compensate by saying she won't be so pernickety in the future (her version of less pernickety: to allow spills…in the sink). Phoebe's answer is important: 'Ah, honey. It's not your fault, you know. This is who you are – and I love you and I want us to be friends. And if I keep living here, I don't see that happening.'

The differences that bond, interest and amuse us in our friends day-to-day take on an entirely new relevance when living together. Monica can't change her controlling nature and for her the passive-aggression is symptomatic of her inability to deal with Phoebe's chaos. These are not things either of them can compromise on and they know it. Pet peeves, preferences and standards of cleanliness are negotiable – character traits are not.

Rachel on the other hand, portrayed as super-easy to live with as she's so laid-back, can deal with it. She and Monica successfully live together for six years, with some minor grumbles, but no major dramas. This is because the things that annoy them can be discussed and worked on: Rachel's laziness with chores being a good example. She doesn't do the washing-up, doesn't know where the trash chute is and hasn't taken the Christmas lights down for months (she argues that Monica should have put a note on the fridge – only for Monica to point out that she has (1.16)). When Rachel moves out so Chandler can move in, Phoebe, in a bid to stop them both being sad, asks them to list bad things about living together (6.06). The worst they can come up with is that Monica cleans the toilet 17 times a day 'Even if people are on it!' and that Rachel forgets to pass on phone messages (remember phone messages?!). Pretty good going really.

The difference between deal-breakers and compromisable annoyances is addressed again in Season 5 when Ross moves in with Chandler and Joey. His infuriating 'quiet down' gesture (you're doing it now aren't you?), his inability to just chill out and his constant need to be *doing* are unbearable for 'Bert and Ernie'. He has to go. And then there are religious, cultural, philosophical (i.e. ethical) and environmental beliefs to consider. As all six friends are white, middle-class New Yorkers who live similar lifestyles, they don't have to contend with these things within their living arrangements, but in the real world they are important factors to keep in mind.

If someone says they can't live with you it doesn't mean they don't love you, just that you're not compatible roommates. Recognize that this isn't a reflection on the depth of the bond you share, but on how well certain traits mesh in the close confines of a shared home.

YOU WILL DISCOVER YOUR FRIENDS ARE GROSS AND ANNOYING

What do we actually know about our friends' hygiene habits, their strange nighttime rituals or their eating customs? Yes, you're aware that your friend Kate enjoys practising yoga. You've even joined her for a class or two. But this is an abstract fact about her that has never impinged on your daily life before. Now that you live together though, you discover she likes to practise in the living room with all the windows open (whatever the weather), for two hours *every single evening* during the exact time you'd usually be settling in for a boxset binge.

When you live with people you learn things about them you'd never have any reason to know otherwise – and those things can be gross and annoying. Phoebe's rat-babies and Joey licking spoons to clean them spring to mind. In 'The One Where Joey Moves Out' (2.16), Chandler and Joey are having breakfast, discussing

CHANDLER: Can. Open. Worms. Everywhere!

how odd it is that Captain Crunch's eyebrows are on his hat, when Joey licks his spoon and throws it back into the drawer. 'Appalled' doesn't convey the depth of Chandler's horror; a horror only exacerbated when he then discovers Joey has also been using his toothbrush…to unclog the drain.

Monica E. Geller*

NICKNAMES/ALIASES: Mon; Fat Monica; Big Fat Goalie; Harmonica; Candy Lady; Crazy Plate Lady.

PARENTS: Jack and Judy Geller.

SIBLINGS: Ross Geller.

NOTABLE RELATIONSHIPS: Kip (we never meet him, but he's the instigator of the 'phase-out' debate); Fun Bobby; Pete; Richard; Chandler.

CHILDREN: Jack and Erica Bing (adopted with Chandler in Season 10).

HISTORY WITH THE FRIENDS: Ross's sister; Rachel's high-school best friend; roommates with Phoebe.

CHILDHOOD: Monica had a difficult relationship with her parents, her brother Ross, and with food while growing up. Her mother, Judy, (unconsciously?) puts her down and favours Ross culminating in a competitiveness between the siblings that shapes many of their childhood interactions. Monica's weight is the subject of many jokes throughout the show that have aged the programme, particularly as she always seems much happier, more carefree and with better mental health in these episodes...so why the fat-shaming?

PROFESSION: Chef at Iridium; waitress at Moondance Diner; food critic; head chef at Alessandro's; head chef at Javu.

KEY FLASHBACK MOMENT: In 'The One That Could Have Been, Part 2' (6.16), Monica loses her virginity to Chandler proving that they would still have ended up together even if history had played out differently.

PERSONALITY: Monica is a caregiver, showing love by providing for others (mostly through food). A neurotic people-pleaser she needs everyone to like her to an anxiety-provoking degree (as when she makes three different types of potatoes for Thanksgiving dinner). She's ambitious, highly competitive, organized, a planner, impatient and controlling – but aware of all of these things. Above all, she's the linchpin (the host and the 'mother hen') around which all the other friends orbit.

* We never discover what the 'E' stands for. In 2.21 she gets obsessed with watching the stock market ticker on TV and invests in a company that has her initials – 'M.E.G.' – but that's as much as we find out.

MEMORABLE QUOTE: 'And remember, if I'm harsh with you, it's only because you're doing it wrong.'

INTERESTING FACT: After Courteney Cox's marriage to David Arquette she changed her name to 'Courteney Cox Arquette'. As a jokey tribute, 'Arquette' was added to every single name that appears on the opening credits of 'The One After Vegas' (6.01).

Hygiene, laziness and different expectations surrounding chores (and even morals!) are incredibly tricky topics to address because they feel deeply personal. Any criticism feels humiliating and so needs to be handled with care.

A perfect example of how not to address a delicate situation can be found in 'The One With Two Parts, Part One' (1.16) when Monica refers to the fact that Rachel hasn't taken the Christmas lights down by saying: 'Ah no, you see, *someone* was supposed to take them down around New Year's, but obviously *someone* forgot.' Being called out, passively-aggressively, in front of the group, is not going to go down well. Here are some other 'don't dos':

- **Don't bring things up in front of a group (pretty much every issue in the show becomes a group discussion: great for comedy moments, not so workable in reality).**
- **Don't outrightly say that what they're doing is disgusting (as Chandler does in the spoon scenario).**
- **Definitely don't infer that what they're doing reflects on their character (as Monica's '*someone*' lines infer Rachel is lazy and/or forgetful).**
- **Don't say that everyone else knows and/or thinks it's wrong too. (One of the most awkward moments of Monica and Rachel's cohabitation occurs when Ross claims 'Monica agrees with me' that he and Rachel were definitely on a break (3.17). People talking about us behind our backs is a universal fear, so it's adding insult to injury).**

So, what should you do?

Take them aside and bring up the issue in private. Act as if it's only a recent thing you've noticed in order to reassure them you haven't been stewing on it for weeks (or months, in the case of Monica and the Christmas lights). And, most importantly, give them an out so they can fix it without you needing to be more direct. For example: 'I've just noticed the Christmas lights are still up. Would you mind taking them down please? Otherwise I will keep forgetting.' Or, 'Do you know why all our spoons seem a bit sticky? I've tried a new washing liquid but it didn't make a difference. Could you make sure you wash the spoons after you use them too?' If they don't get the hint after that, you're going to have to bite the bullet: 'I'm sorry, but the spoons are still really sticky. Could you wash them please?'

Some good tricks for broaching these kind of things include: softening your comments by removing the accusatory 'you' or the passive-aggressive '*someone*' and making it more general; inserting 'I feel' and 'I think' in front of opinions rather than stating them as facts (opinions are never facts – always be clear on the difference); putting the impetus on yourself; and removing any instance of the hyperbolic words 'always' or 'never', so:

- **'There's a smell in the apartment' rather than 'You've stunk up the apartment'.**
- **'I think it's a bit gross' (opinion) rather than 'It is a bit gross' (opinion stated as fact).**
- **'I think I may not have explained how much this bothers me' rather than 'You're ignoring me, which is rude'.**

WHAT KIND OF ROOMMATE ARE YOU?

Which statements do you most agree with? Make a note of your answer (A, B, C or D) then see page 58 to find out what kind of roommate you are.

Your roommate leaves angry notes on their food:

A: I don't care. I'll make food so much better than theirs they'll be begging to eat mine instead.
B: I'm not getting involved.
C: Wait – we're meant to read them? I just threw them away.
D: Yeah, that was me. Stay away from my sandwich.

Your roommate brings back a chick and a duck as pets:

A: Pets...in my house? Without asking me? Are you drunk?
B: As long as I'm not responsible for them, I don't mind.
C: This is awesome. We're going to be poultry parents.
D: I'm going to quietly give them away to a nice farm when they're not around.

Your roommate buys you and them a BarcaLounger each:

A: Omg. Get them out of my beautiful living room.
B: Pretty cool – but can I exchange it?
C: It's the best thing that ever happened to me.
D: Nice idea, but what's the chairs' history? Are they antiques? Do they have a story?

Your roommate is being passive-aggressive about cleaning:

A: Don't blame them. It's infuriating when people don't adhere to the rota.
B: I don't know why. It's not my turn. Is it?
C: I've got just the joke for this situation.
D: I'd rather they were aggressive to be fair, at least that's more straightforward.

All your mates have keys to your pad and you're going on holiday:

A: I'll ask for them back. I don't trust those fools in my place when I'm not there.
B: My roommate is the boss: if they gave out keys, that's their responsibility.
C: Of course they do, how else would the chick and the duck get fed?
D: Doesn't matter, they are welcome to pop in, but my place isn't where people congregate.

RESULTS

Mostly As: MONICA

You're a great roommate – as long as whoever you live with abides by your rules. And you have plenty of them. Sure, you're a bit bossy, but you balance that out by being an incredibly generous host.

Mostly Bs: RACHEL

You'll happily let the alpha roommate rule the roost for an easy life. You'd much prefer someone telling you when and what to clean than being expected to take the initiative. It's nice having a lovely home without taking much responsibility for it.

Mostly Cs: CHANDLER AND JOEY

Your priorities are to have fun, in a reasonably clean space, with someone who makes you laugh and that you want to hang out with. You won't make a big deal out of small things for the overall benefit of a relaxed living situation.

Mostly Ds: PHOEBE AND ROSS

You're a tidy and quiet roommate who respects people's space and would rather talk about disagreements than let them fester. You know what you like and what you don't – and actually, what you'd like most is to live by yourself, surrounded by your own things, without having to deal with anyone else's crap.

The other person has less opportunity to get defensive if you're only stating the (genuine) facts and your feelings about them. Also, using 'always' and 'never' is a failsafe way to minimize any point you're trying to make because a) it's probably untrue and b) the person will go out of their way to find the one instance when they either did or didn't do exactly what you're referring to. Don't give them the opportunity.

Give them a, um, sandwich

A common management trick to soften the delivery of a criticism or simply bad news is to sandwich the negative within two positives (what's commonly known as a 'shit sandwich'). While not about cohabitation specifically, Phoebe uses this tactic to tell Rachel that crapweasel Paolo made a pass at her (1.12). Phoebe explains that there are three things Rachel should know about her: that her friends are the most important things in her life (a positive!), that she never lies (Paolo made a pass at her) and that she makes the best oatmeal raisin cookies in the world (hurray!). She sandwiches the Paolo blow between love and cookies – surely better than hearing the news with no 'bread' at all?

ASK BEFORE BORROWING AND REPLACE WHAT YOU USE (OR LOSE)

In 'The One Where Ross Can't Flirt' (5.19), Rachel panics when she finds out that the earring she's lost is Monica's rather than Phoebe's because she's 'not allowed to borrow her stuff'. This is a nice insight into a conversation Monica and Rachel must have had off-screen establishing 'rules' for their friendship – the kind of rules that are essential when you live together. They both clearly know that if Rachel keeps borrowing things and losing them it'll cause irreparable damage to their set-up. This is something they've acknowledged, agreed and acted upon.

Asking before you borrow something and replacing things you've used or lost sounds obvious. Not so! Take the time Rachel 'borrows' Hugsy, Joey's beloved cuddly toy penguin, to give to her daughter Emma. Joey is (let's not beat around the bush) distraught. He even buys another one for Emma so he can keep the original. Rachel's dismissiveness of Joey's feelings is decidedly not cool for a roommate. We're all weird and have our eccentricities. While Rachel finds it odd that Joey is so attached to Hugsy, that's actually none of her business. She should accept it and move on. Emma having the toy genuinely creates friction between the friends and leads both to feel embarrassed: Joey for caring so much about Hugsy and Rachel over Joey's seemingly uncharacteristic meanness. Had she asked if she could borrow him beforehand, the situation could have been avoided.

RESPECT EVERYONE'S SPACE

Respecting someone's right to privacy is the bedrock upon which successful co-living is built. Everyone needs somewhere they can dance around naked singing into a loofah without fear of judgement or interruption (no Ross, Rachel is not sending you a coded invite for sex through the goddam window (5.23)).

You cannot trespass into someone's space by spying, listening or breaking in. The end. Them's the rules. Get out. When Rachel and Phoebe convince Chandler they should all try to find Monica's Christmas present hiding space (6.10) and then when Chandler breaks open Monica's 'secret closet' (8.14), no one comes out of either scenario well. Rachel and Phoebe admit that on previous hunts they've found Chandler's badly hidden porn stash, Monica's trust is violated and everyone ends up feeling generally quite grubby and sheepish.

Asking before you borrow something fits into this category too, as to borrow you'll 'trespass' into someone's territory – be it a wardrobe, fridge or bedroom. How trespass is dealt with depends upon common courtesy and personal expectation. Chandler's roommate Eddie (who moves in after Joey leaves to live on his own in Season 2), laughs in the face of personal space, even watching Chandler as he sleeps. This is an extreme example of a very real issue. Personal

boundaries are essential when you live together – any rules that existed previously in non-roommate times no longer apply. So while yes, you may have regularly rooted through your friend's wardrobe before while getting ready for nights out, it's an entirely different proposition to do so again now that you live together.

Respecting space also covers communal areas. Having parties every evening, playing your ukulele at midnight, buying a hairless cat (*cough* Rachel) or taking up the living room for your two-hour daily yoga sesh – none of these things are okay. Same goes with interrupting your friends' dinner plans by wandering in uninvited, grabbing a plate and pulling up a chair (like Ross and Rachel do when Monica and Chandler are having dinner with Phoebe and Mike (10.14)).

Of course spontaneous gatherings or parties may happen, that's a given when living with other people, but the general rule must be: don't push it. If what you're doing directly impacts your roommate, that fact must be acknowledged. Same goes for having partners over. Quietly moving them in without addressing it is terrible roommate etiquette, as illustrated by Monica's fury over always finding Ross in her space in Season 2: 'He's here when I go to sleep. He's here when I wake up. He's here when I want to use the shower!' Either agree said partner is essentially another roommate and so will need to pay a share of the bills, or agree they can't be around *all the freaking time*.

MAKE RULES FOR SHARING FOOD AND CHORES

Sharing food, eating together and cooking for others are all running themes throughout the show – and rightly so. How you eat and who you eat with is of great societal and cultural importance everywhere. An entire psychology book could be written about Monica's relationship with food but, suffice to say here: she enjoys feeding people and cooking gives her comfort (even when it goes too far – remember the Halloween candy episode? (7.09)). However, Monica has got herself in a situation where she's set a precedent she can't easily back out of. Because she's always allowed everyone to eat from her fridge and never said anything, it'll be tough now to instil new rules…but not impossible.

When it comes to sharing food in a co-living space, setting boundaries is important. Channel your inner Joey: 'Joey doesn't share food'; or your inner Ross with aggressive notes taped to his sandwiches. While these examples play out badly in the show, in reality labelling food (with labels that aren't pass-agg or just downright agg) may be necessary if you find it a simpler way of establishing your own preferences (particularly relevant if there's lots of people sharing a kitchen). Otherwise, agree on what is and isn't fair game for sharing and also whether you'll have a kitty for the items that are. The only thing that is non-negotiable is that you…

TALK ABOUT IT BEFORE YOU EXPLODE

Stewing on things and building them up in your head
will lead to an eventual explosion and then *you'll* be in the
wrong. Your reaction will seem totally out of proportion to
the 'crime'. We're all guilty of snapping over something
inconsequential and then feeling infuriated when the person
we're snapping at flags up how ridiculous it seems. In reality,
the explosion is the result of a cumulation of annoyances,
peeves and perceived slights that have built up into
incontrovertible evidence of rudeness and disrespect. The
culprit, however, will usually be totally oblivious (as you've
never said anything and they can't read your mind) and so will
justifiably be surprised and annoyed at what can only be
viewed as a gross over-reaction.

To stop this happening, talk seriously about pet peeves or
things you generally can't put up with no matter how seemingly
inconsequential. Also, make sure the person you're telling
realizes that you are serious. Saying 'Hey, don't lick the spoons'
in an off-hand way may seem like a joke to someone who
doesn't know that licking spoons isn't an alternative way of
cleaning them (2.16).

The importance of open and honest conversations cannot be
underplayed when living together. Essentially *Friends* is a
recurring comedy of errors where assumptions and secrets
lead to calamitous scenarios. Hilarious to watch, *awful* to live
through. Some of the funniest scenes are those where we
watch characters lose their minds after one final tiny thing tips
them over the edge (*whispers* Ross's 'moist-maker' sandwich

(5.9) or Joey's date taking his fries (10.9)). To the person being exploded at, it seems like madness. Who could possibly be so upset about a sandwich or nicking a fry? Ahem, *everyone*. We all have pet peeves, things that really wind us up, be they totally 'normal' or seemingly ludicrous to other people.

How and when you talk about these things can be the difference between a friendship-defining explosion or a civilized and helpful chat. The way Chandler and Joey deal with Joey's snoring is an excellent example of a healthy friend-come-roommate solution to a problem (4.20). Joey's snoring is a huge deal for Chandler, affecting his daily life, so Joey agrees to go to a sleep clinic and ends up having to wear a mouthguard in bed. He doesn't ignore the problem or tell Chandler to get over it – an example of why they're such successful roommates.

DON'T TAKE THINGS PERSONALLY

Here's news: not everyone lives by the same 'rules'. We all have different expectations and standards when it comes to behavioural norms. What you find incredibly irritating or rude, someone else may not care about in the slightest. Say, like Monica, you always wash up immediately after eating and would never dream of leaving it overnight. However, your friend (ahem, Rachel) prefers to tackle it the next day (or not at all). You end up doing it for them… night after night after night. Inevitably you begin to take this personally: they *must know* you're going to do it. So, what – they're just expecting you to do it for them?! How rude! How awful! This is so typical of *them*! Undoubtedly some of these thoughts are running through Monica's mind as she fumes in the coffee house knowing Rachel still won't have washed the dishes upon her return home.

It's easy to see how things like this can spiral, but so many of these issues are simply misunderstandings caused by the belief that because you wouldn't do something, no other reasonable person would either. In reality, the fact your friend leaves the washing-up most likely has absolutely *nothing to do with you*. They just prefer to do it in the morning. It's like when Joey discovers Phoebe and Rachel have ordered pizza without him when he's in London (4.24). He can't believe it – but it never crossed their minds that he'd be sad about it.

Acknowledging that people don't live by the same rules makes life so much easier, releasing you from the anxiety of taking things personally. We constantly relate everything people do back to ourselves ('How could they do this to me?'), when the truth is, most people are only thinking about themselves too. When you live together, rather than ruminate on perceived slights or insults until you're furious, try talking about it and making compromises. Don't dismiss other people's 'rules', accept them and work around them.

MAKE PLANS TOGETHER OUTSIDE YOUR HOME

One of the best things about the series is how much the group *do* together. They regularly go to the theatre, Knicks games, the movies, out to lunch or on mini-breaks. When you live with friends it can be easy to think you already spend lots of time hanging out in your home so don't need to make any extra effort. Not true. Discussing whose turn it is to buy toilet paper is not the same as spending a day at the beach, going to a festival or heading out to dinner.

Making *proper* time for each other will ensure your friendship doesn't get relegated to 'just roommates' status. It will also remind you why you're friends in the first place, as well as easing the transition when one of you moves out.

It can be incredibly difficult to tell a close friend that you're leaving a beloved shared home. *Friends* deals with this several times over the course of its ten-year run: when Joey leaves Chandler to try living on his own, when Chandler leaves Joey to move in with Monica (thus also de-homing Rachel) and, as already mentioned, when Phoebe moves out of Monica's (twice!). It's always going to be the end of an era when you've shared such close confines with someone for any period of time. Either the person leaving or the person left may feel

conflicted about the decision and nervous about what it means for the friendship going forward. Marking the occasion and not playing it down is important – as shown by Chandler and Joey's misunderstanding regarding Joey moving out. Their determinedly cavalier response to the event results in neither one of them admitting they want to go back to how things were. Friendship is defined by the ability to be vulnerable with each other. Moving out (or moving in) demands an expectation of vulnerability and there's no point denying that or underplaying it. You will see each other at your weirdest, grossest, saddest, nakedest (especially if you never lock the bathroom door like the gang don't seem to), and happiest. Losing that closeness is a big deal so make sure you celebrate the end of an era in style.

LESSONS LEARNED

- Just because you aren't good roommates doesn't mean you're not good friends.

- Respecting each other's space, and understanding each other's idiosyncrasies and 'rules' is essential for successful cohabitation.

- Talk before you explode and don't take things personally. Most 'dramas' can be defused by a simple honest conversation.

CHAPTER 4

THE ONE WITH ALL THE DATING

'How you doin'?'

Friends is, at its heart, a love story — between the group as a whole, but with the main romantic focus on Ross and Rachel. Their will-they-won't-they relationship is the thread holding the ten seasons together. Chandler and Monica's love affair, while entirely satisfying, is a mere side dish to the Ross and Rachel main course. The dysfunctional pair are the 'moist-maker' of the show if you will (apologies, for some reason we can't stop saying 'moist-maker'). However, rather than providing lessons on how to pursue love, viewers are far more likely to use their relationship as a step-by-step guide on what not to do. And they aren't, by any means, the only ones. All the characters run the gamut of dating pitfalls, whether looking for casual sex or meaningful connections. And thank goodness for that because it means we can laugh at their mistakes, tell ourselves we'd never do the same and then promptly follow exactly in their footsteps.

Here are the key dating lessons we can take from the show.

ALWAYS ABIDE BY 'THE CODE'

'The Code', referred to several times throughout the show, refers to the unwritten but sacred rules of friendship. This code helps friends navigate ethically dubious situations; without it there would be no trust. It's about mutual respect, prioritizing boundaries and everyone being equal. You may learn your friends have stricter expectations of The Code than you do when you suddenly find yourself on the wrong side of it, however, that's part of a healthy debate.

Phoebe and Joey realize they have different expectations of The Code when Joey cancels their dinner to go on a date in 'The One With All The Cheesecakes' (7.11). What is never under discussion though, is the existence of The Code in the first place. You may stretch the rules to suit yourself sometimes, but all pals must acknowledge its existence as the moral baseline for successful friendships. The Code isn't only about romance; there are unwritten friendship rules for everything. However, the reason it's appearing in this chapter is because sex and romance inevitably veer into grey areas. When it comes to matters of the heart, things get complicated – essentially we're all liable to lose our minds and behave in ways we otherwise wouldn't dream of. Some of the show's biggest inter-group dramas are caused by romance betrayals – a betrayal being defined as breaking The Code: letting your friend down in a way that shakes the foundation of your friendship. When it comes to dating, we all learn the hard way that The Code is not to be messed with.

JOEY: Hey! You can cancel plans with friends if there's a possibility for sex.

ROSS: Phoebe, he's right. That is the rule.

PHOEBE: I don't accept this rule! When we make plans, I expect you to show up.

The Code According to Friends

- **You cannot kiss your friend's other half.** When Chandler kisses Kathy, Joey's girlfriend, it turns into one of the most infamous betrayals on the show (4.07). It's even more heart-rending because Joey had agreed they could date after Chandler asked for his blessing, not realizing he'd already gone behind his back. Into the apology box you go, Chandler!

- **Exes are off-limits** – except in ex-ceptional (sorry) circumstances (see above). If you do accidentally sleep with your friend's ex, you have to fess up and take the heat just like Ross does after hooking up with Janice in 'The One With Chandler's Work Laugh' (5.12). The response you'll get is dependent on many factors: the depth of feeling between the exes, the length of their relationship and how bad their break-up was. Then there's also the situation that led you to break The Code: was it a drunken one-night thing or do you actually have feelings for the person? You may get lucky and receive a Chandler response, aka they think it's hilarious, or you may find yourself in a friendship-ending nightmare à la Joey and Ross who is just 'FINE' about Joey and Rachel, by the way (10.02). Exes are best avoided like the plague unless you're prepared to jeopardize a friendship.

- **You are allowed to cancel dinner plans** with your friend only if you're meeting up with a long-lost love who's back from Minsk for one night only.

- **You must tell your friend if you think their partner is cheating.** They not only deserve to know, but will be mortified to discover later that no one told them. Phoebe does the right thing in telling Rachel that Paolo made a pass at her in Season 1, Joey steps up when he catches Janice kissing her ex in Season 3 and the whole group get friendship props in Season 10 for telling Monica they think Chandler's doing the dirty.

- **You cannot kiss either of your friend's parents.** There are no exceptions. No, it doesn't matter if they're a super-hot erotica author who hits on you first. Stand strong, leave the situation.

- **You cannot set up your friend's ex** with another friend, even if they say it's fine. Despite Rachel claiming she's okay with it, Phoebe setting Ross up with Bonnie in Season 3 kick-starts a chain reaction of events that doesn't end well for anyone – least of all for Bonnie's hair.

- **You can date someone both you and your friend fancy** as long as you're open about it. This goes against The Code, but hear us out. In 'The One After the Superbowl, Part 2' (2.13),

Monica tells Rachel she fancies Jean-Claude Van Damme, who's starring in a movie shooting in New York. However, he asks Rachel out instead. Rachel asks Monica if it's okay and she says yes. So far, so good – this is excellent Code-following behaviour. However, then the show gets it wrong. There's no way real friends would hold a terrible grudge over this, let alone end up in a hair-pulling fight as the characters do. Monica has never even met the guy, why would she resent Rachel going out with him? A non-reciprocated crush does not dictate future romance. This storyline is even more ludicrous considering Joey was fine (in the end) with Chandler dating his actual ex-girlfriend.

- **Don't play the 'Who would you date in the group?' game.** When Monica asks who Phoebe and Rachel would date out of the three of them (6.12), both she and Rachel sensibly say they don't know, but Phoebe immediately replies 'Rachel'. It would have been less stressful to poke an angry bear with a big stick.

- **Don't drunkenly hook up with one of your friend's siblings** if it means nothing and you'll barely remember it the next day. Especially don't do it if they're one of seven and you can't remember which one it was (who wants to challenge Chandler to another round of 'try to pick Mary-Angela out of a line-up'? We do!).

TWO FRIENDS DATING AFFECTS THE WHOLE GROUP

If two people within your friendship group hook up, don't kid yourself that it won't affect the group dynamic. When Rachel and Ross first split up after the 'We were on a break!' debacle, things are so acrimonious that the gang introduces a first come, first served policy as regards to who gets dibs on group activities. This leads Rachel and Ross to pre-book the others weeks in advance so as not to miss out, and leaves everyone else feeling guilty about whoever's left behind. The situation comes to a head in 'The One Without the Ski Trip' (3.17), when Rachel's plan for a weekend away (sans Ross) flounders after their car breaks down and Ross has to rescue them. The ridiculousness of the situation instigates an honest chat about how much it's affecting the group and prompts the ex-couple to agree to try to be civil. Whether this civility would succeed or not in reality is open to debate, especially considering Ross is always at Monica's, aka Rachel's, apartment.

But even if the relationship works out for the best, it will change things within the group in lots of other ways. Chandler and Monica's romance alters, among other things: how much time Chandler spends with Joey, the living set-up for two

households, the relationship between Chandler and Ross (now potential brothers-in-law) and what the group can discuss regarding dating and sex.

The lesson here is clear: don't enter into a relationship with a close friend without considering the implication on the group as a whole. It shouldn't stop you, but you must recognize the inevitable impact, be sensitive to it and be prepared to swallow your pride and heartbreak for the good of the gang if things go south.

SEX WITH A FRIEND IS COMPLICATED

When Rachel and Ross conceive Emma, they want everyone to believe that the sex was just a one-off, a one-time thing, a bit of fun between two people who've rolled around naked together lots of times before. This, as everyone knows, is total rubbish. It's clear, with all their history, that it's part of the inevitable build-up to Phoebe finally being proved right that Rachel is indeed Ross's lobster.

Meanwhile though, casual hooking up with friends is broached again, this time during 'The One With the Soap Opera Party'

Take Advantage of the Free Sex Advice

One of the best things about dating is revealing horror stories to your pals, laughing over terrible choices and asking for genuine advice. *Friends* covers some classic OMG scenarios including:

- When your friend dates someone much younger than them. (Monica)
- When your friend dates someone much older than them. (Monica)
- When your friend gets dumped because they have a third nipple. (Chandler)
- When your friend has slept with everybody in town. (Joey)
- When your friend is dating their student. (Ross)
- When your friend is dating someone purely for the 'animal sex'. (Rachel)
- When your friend is dating two people at once. (Phoebe and Joey)

Realizing that everyone has had good, bad and AWFUL experiences is entirely reassuring as well as hilarious. Speaking about this stuff is liberating and something we should all do more of. It's free advice about things that are no doubt much more common than you think. And, who knows, after your friend's explained the seven erogenous zones to you (4.11), it may just change your (sex) life.

(9.20). When Rachel announces to Monica that she's going to try to kiss Joey, Monica warns her: 'Friends hooking up is a bad idea'. And she should know, having slept with Chandler just for fun…and then ending up marrying the guy.

Assuming that friends fooling around will be complication-free is misguided. The main difference between a friendship and a romantic relationship is typically physical intimacy, therefore crossing that line isn't simple. How people feel about the importance of sex and what it means is entirely personal, which can lead to confusion between friends about what the act meant. Sex is intimate (that's the whole point of it), so to know your friend in that way can change how you perceive them and how you perceive your relationship. For someone who thinks of sex as entirely casual and has multiple partners, having sex with a friend who views it as special may cause problems. And, even if you both agree upfront that it will be relaxed, experiencing a hot and heavy night with someone you care about may change things for you after the fact. Careful boundaries need to be set, such as: no sleepovers, no flirting with other people in front of each other (or alternatively, no jealousy about flirting in front of each other) and always being open and honest about what's cool and what's not.

Friends with benefits can work, but only if you're both on the same page. As soon as one of you isn't, maintaining the friendship needs to take priority and the sex needs to stop.

AVOID KNEE-JERK REACTIONS TO YOUR FRIEND'S PARTNERS

What's the best thing to do if you dislike a friend's partner? It's not that they've done anything wrong, they're just not one of you. Do you suck it up or say something? This awkward scenario is brilliantly played out when Phoebe dates irritating psychiatrist Roger in Season 1. His on-the-nose analysis of everyone in the group gets their backs up to such a degree that they all acknowledge that they hate him and end up telling Phoebe, who gets mad…and then concedes they're right. In reality, this is a terrible way of dealing with things. Knowing your friends have been talking about someone you care about behind your back is hurtful. Also, as this is someone you've chosen to be with, you'd be forgiven for wondering what that choice says about you and understandably become defensive. And then there's the cringe factor of now knowing everyone dislikes him, but you're choosing to stay with him. An intolerable situation that will inevitably lead to a natural drifting apart (either between you and your pals, or you and whoever you are dating).

You've got to ask yourself what you want to achieve in telling someone you don't like their other half. Interjecting yourself into someone's life in such a way is a big deal, so run these questions past yourself first:

- **Could your dislike be more about you than them? For example, now your friend is less available to you, are you actually projecting sadness over that loss on to the interloper who has stolen them away?**

- **Might you be jealous of their happiness?** This isn't a nice thing to realize about yourself but it's important to consider. If you're feeling competitive with your friend and want what they have, you may be subconsciously (or worse, consciously) attempting to damage their relationship in the hope that you can both return to the same stage in life.

- **Are you judging this person based upon your own standards?** Remember, you are not your friend. We all like different things. You don't get to dictate who people love (a shame), so if they're not hurting your friend but are actually making them happy, it's time to pipe down.

If the answer to all of the above is 'no', it's still not time to say anything. Instead, try to get to know their partner better. They may have given a bad first impression — remember it's intimidating meeting close friends for the first time. Give them another chance. Maybe even spend some one-on-one time together like Joey and Janice attempt in Season 3. If nothing else, your friend will appreciate the effort. If you're still not keen, make sure you book some regular time in with your friend alone so you don't always have to share them. Only tell your friend if they ask or if it becomes painfully obvious, and then be gentle, qualifying the statement with the truth: 'But I'm not dating them so it doesn't matter. As long as they make you happy.' Your friend also has to accept that you won't automatically love who they love and that's life. Ross has absolutely nothing to say to Phoebe's boyfriend Mike, yet neither of them let that affect their relationships with Phoebe. Ross can see Mike makes her happy — and that's all we want for our friends, isn't it?

Joseph 'Joey' Francis Tribbiani Jr.

NICKNAMES/ALIASES: Dr. Drake Ramoray; Ken Adams; Joseph Stalin; Dragon; Chick; Joe; VD Boy.

PARENTS: Joey Tribbiani Sr. and Gloria Tribbiani.

SIBLINGS: Seven sisters (just don't ask Chandler which one is Mary-Angela).

RELATIONSHIPS: Too many. Notable mentions: Rachel; Kathy; Janine; Charlie.

CHILDREN: Surrogate step-father to Emma, Rachel and Ross's baby.

HISTORY WITH THE FRIENDS: Joins the gang after becoming Chandler's roommate.

CHILDHOOD: From a close-knit Italian-American family of eight kids, Joey is very protective of all his sisters. He's devastated when he finds out his father has a long-term mistress…and then surprised to discover his mum is fine with it. As a young boy he had an imaginary friend called Maurice who was a space cowboy.

PROFESSION: Actor; cologne sampler; entry-level processor (at Chandler's company); acting teacher;

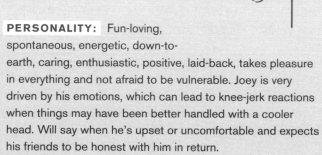

Christmas-tree salesman; museum tour guide; waiter.

KEY FLASHBACK MOMENT:

When Joey is newly moved in with Chandler, he thinks the hot woman across the hall, Monica, is trying it on with him and strips naked in her living room. Monica has seen Joey naked! No one ever mentions this again. (3.06).

PERSONALITY: Fun-loving,

spontaneous, energetic, down-to-earth, caring, enthusiastic, positive, laid-back, takes pleasure in everything and not afraid to be vulnerable. Joey is very driven by his emotions, which can lead to knee-jerk reactions when things may have been better handled with a cooler head. Will say when he's upset or uncomfortable and expects his friends to be honest with him in return.

MEMORABLE QUOTE: 'You don't own a TV? What's all your furniture pointed at?'

INTERESTING FACT: In 2015, Matt LeBlanc revealed on an episode of the UK TV series, *The Graham Norton Show*, that 'there is a new crop of teenagers finding it [*Friends*] for the first time. They say [to me], "What's with the grey hair? Are you Joey's dad?"'

BUT DO STEP IN IF SOMETHING'S NOT RIGHT

It's a totally different scenario, however, if your friend's partner is actually hurting your friend or behaving in a way you see as detrimental to their happiness. (If you believe they're being abused, either physically or emotionally, please visit the websites listed on page 159 for advice.) When Ross says Rachel's name at the altar (GOOD GOD, MAN!), Emily lays out some ground rules for him to follow so they can try to salvage their marriage. The group tries to be understanding at first and not to interfere…but soon realize things are going too far. It's one thing for Ross to agree not to see Rachel (also not cool), but when they discover he's also consented to move uptown and sell all of his belongings, they decide they need to say something. It takes this intervention for him to realize that yes, while he did make a terrible mistake, he doesn't want to live this way.

Sensitivity is integral in dishing out this kind of news. Obviously it depends on the seriousness of the situation and your relationship with your friend, but following the below guidelines will help:

- Do it face to face. Text messages can be misconstrued and you can't read tone. You want to be present to comfort them and show you care.
- Take them somewhere private where they can react without fear of public embarrassment. (The group do it in Ross's apartment so he's in a safe space.)
- Don't gang up on them or make them feel this is an us and you situation. (Ross feels entirely ganged upon. Chandler, Monica, Joey and Phoebe all tell him

together. It would have been so much better if one of them had taken him aside.)

- Have proof for your concerns. Don't make accusations if you can't back them up. The first thing they're going to ask is why you're saying this. It's a fair question. Have examples, such as changes in their behaviour over time. (They list the changes Ross's agreed to, mention that they seem extreme and also question whether this will make him happy.)

On another note: Ross's behaviour towards Rachel leaves a lot to be desired throughout the whole show – and it's only raised a couple of times by the rest of the group. He tells Paolo he and she are dating when they're not (1.07); he 'saves' her from a flirty conversation with a guy she's enjoying, though he is not dating Rachel at the time (2.14); he doesn't give her the message from a man she gave her number to (9.09) – the list goes on. Hurray for Phoebe then, who flags up his controlling nature in Season 2. When Ross says he doesn't like tattoos, Rachel starts backing out of her plan with Phoebe to get one – a plan she'd previously been excited about.

> PHOEBE: I don't believe this. Is this how this relationship's gonna work? Ross equals boss? I mean, come on. What is this – 1922?

Friendship questions you never thought you'd have to ask yourself

Friendship is a funny beast. There you are, enjoying a perfectly normal day, probably debating eating another sandwich, when suddenly your friend arrives breathless at the door clasping what he claims is your mutual mate's professional porn film in his hands. What to do? *Friends* showed us that in long-term friendships anything is possible. Below are some questions it's worth considering now so you're fully-prepared when the totally unexpected happens.

Would you forgive your friend if they mugged you in the past?

Imagine one of your most traumatic childhood experiences was being mugged outside a comic-book store by a pipe-waving lunatic who stole your hand-drawn artwork for your original story 'Science Boy' (superpower: 'a superhuman thirst for knowledge'). Imagine then discovering the mugger was now one of your best friends. Could you forgive them? How about if they revealed they'd kept 'Science Boy' all this time? (9.15)

Would you pee on your friend if they were stung by a jellyfish?

You and a group of pals are messing about on the beach on a blissfully hot day when suddenly one screams in agony. They've been stung by a jellyfish. One of you has to step up (or crouch down) to help them in this hour of need. Do you offer your services? And, if you're the one who's been stung, do you accept said services? Could you ever look each other in the face again?

Would you watch your friend's sex tape?

This question comes up several times in the show (surprising considering the effort it took to make home movies back in the 90s): when everyone wants to discover who initiated things between Ross and Rachel when they conceived Emma (8.04); when Chandler and Joey discover a tape titled 'Monica' in her ex Richard's apartment (9.07); and when, most horrifically, Monica accidentally catches the end of her parents' sex tape when watching an old prom video (2.14). If you discovered a sex tape your friend had made, would you watch it? And, if you did, would you admit that you had?

Would you watch your friend's professional porn film?

When Joey discovers Phoebe's a porn star and rents 'Buffay the Vampire Layer' from the adult movie store, the rest of the gang can't wait to watch her performance; only Joey refuses: 'This is wrong, you guys – Phoebe's our friend!' (6.14) It's only upon learning it's her twin sister Ursula that Joey pulls up a chair. Does it feel slightly less creepy because it's a publicly available film rather than a privately made sex tape? And if so, would you watch it?

Would you bet your apartment that you know your friends better than they know you?

How well do you think you know your pals? Well enough that you'd bet your beautiful apartment on it? Monica's competitiveness definitely contributes to this rash decision on her part, but it's her absolute conviction that she and Rachel know Chandler and Joey inside out that seals the deal (4.12). She's utterly convinced – and she's wrong. Would you make that bet? Do you think you know your friends better than they know you?

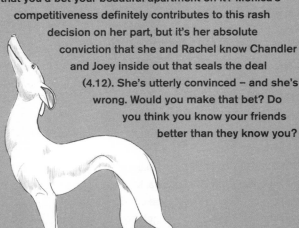

This comes after Phoebe heard Rachel tell Ross: 'I fell for you and I get clobbered. You then fall for me and I, again, somehow get clobbered' (2.14) – a wake-up call to anyone listening in that there's inequality in the relationship. One of the biggest friend-fails regarding this though, was how no one stepped in regarding his brazenly problematic jealousy over Rachel's colleague Mark, despite the impact it was having on Rachel's life. If your friend mentions negative things about their partner several times and/or you see it impacting their life (as the gang does with Ross's jealousy or the times he interferes in Rachel's relationships with other guys), don't be scared to flag it up to your pal like Phoebe does. Let them know you've clocked it and are open to speaking about it.

BREAK-UPS SUCK

Whether you're the dumpee, the dumped or one half of a 'mutual decision', breaking up is categorically awful. The show highlights some special cases too: when someone you love doesn't love you back (Phoebe's actually-not-gay-after-all green-card husband, Duncan Sullivan), when you have to break up even though you still love each other (Monica and Richard, Phoebe and David) and when your husband says someone else's name at your wedding (Emily, we're sorry).

Whether you deal with it by making truckloads of jam like Monica, by going to a strip club and eating 'the good ice cream' like Chandler, or by getting yourself a pet monkey like Ross, one thing's for sure, you'll need your friends

to be sympathetic, patient and non-judgemental about the undoubtedly terrible decisions you're going to make (such as Rachel returning to cheater Paolo in a misguided attempt to get over Ross (2.01)).

FRIENDSHIP IS MORE IMPORTANT THAN ROMANCE

Friends come first. When Joey's roommate-come-girlfriend Janine (Elle Macpherson) admits to not liking Monica and Chandler it doesn't take long for Joey to decide she's got to go. Just as when Phoebe tells Rachel that Paolo hit on her, Rachel doesn't doubt it for a moment, but instead, actually apologizes to Phoebe for bringing such a creep into their lives (an unnecessary apology, but a very sweet one). And, one of the best examples of putting your pals first is undoubtedly when Chandler gives Joey the incredibly thoughtful present he bought for Kathy so Joey can impress her (yes, he ruins this gesture spectacularly by kissing her – but the initial thought was solid). The love between friends outranks that shared between romantic entanglements. This sentiment is echoed in Monica's wedding vows to Chandler: 'my prince, my soul mate, my friend' (7.24). An important distinction, for not all romantic partners act as good friends and friendship is a bond that lasts for ever (as long as you abide by The Code).

LESSONS LEARNED

- The Code is law when it comes to, well, everything to do with friendship, but it's particularly important when you enter any kind of romantic grey zone. Always abide by the rules – because friendship is more important than romance.

- Sex and love are complicated. Make sure you enter any friends-with-benefits scenario or romance with a pal with your eyes wide open.

- Talk, gossip, compare notes and cry on numerous shoulders: one of the best things about friendship is how tears turn to laughter when faced with messy romantic situations.

CHAPTER 5
THE ONE WITH THE MONEY PROBLEMS

'I learned never to borrow money from friends. No, that's why Richard Dreyfuss and I don't speak anymore.'

Phoebe, 'The One Where Rachel Goes Back to Work' (9.11)

Okay, let's cut to the chase here: *Friends* never successfully deals with the issue of money. It doesn't ignore it — money or the lack thereof is actually the subject of many storylines throughout the ten seasons — but it's either always played for laughs (go figure, it is a sitcom), or the awkwardness is emphasized without providing any actionable advice. This is a big shame because how much cash you have is an inevitable component of friendships. Money matters. Unless you live on *The Beach* (hello, bonus Gen X cultural reference!), what's in your bank account dictates how you spend your time. All of your time: where you work, who you work for, how often you work, what you do in your downtime, where you live, what food you eat and so on.

Societally, many of us find it difficult to discuss money. There's many reasons for this, including sensibilities surrounding class, self-worth, gender, race, religion, culture, ambition and privilege. In a world where being rich is historically equated with success, there's a stigma attached to struggling financially. Being honest about money means making yourself vulnerable. However, it's essential that you can have open conversations with close friends about something so integral to your day-to-day life. Not doing so makes experiencing your own version of 'The One With Five Steaks and an Eggplant' (2.05) inevitable.

THE MOST EXCRUCIATING EPISODE EVER

Every fan of the show will remember the aforementioned episode, despite no doubt repeated attempts to erase it from memory. Why? Because it painfully addresses a scenario we're all familiar with, whether we are sitting on the 'rich friends' or 'poor friends' side of the table (a literal table in this instance).

It all starts when Chandler announces to the group that everyone owes him $62 for Ross's birthday celebrations. While acknowledging it is a 'little steep', he justifies the expense with the entirely inappropriate 'But…it's Ross.' (There's so much wrong with this, but hold fire! We're not nearly at the dissecting stage yet.) Monica, Ross and Chandler then all agree the group should go 'someplace nice' for dinner to celebrate Monica being promoted. Rachel orders a side salad (on the side of her glass of water), Joey goes for the Thai chicken pizza and asks whether it's cheaper without the 'nuts and leeks and stuff' and Phoebe orders a cup of the cucumber soup 'and…um…take care'. When Ross splits the bill equally between six, calculating that everyone owes $28, a shocked Rachel asks, 'Wha-, um, everyone…?' Misconstruing her point, Ross then divides it by five instead, so Monica doesn't have to pay on her 'big night'. And that's when the proverbial shit hits the proverbial fan. Phoebe says 'No way! Sorry – not gonna happen!' and explains how she, Rachel and Joey shouldn't have to pay full-

whack for their teeny-tiny food. A decidedly uncomfortable, but very important conversation then takes place in which the poor friends explain to the rich friends that they don't seem to appreciate that they don't have as much disposable cash. The fact that Chandler organized an outing to Hootie & the Blowfish for Ross's birthday is also addressed – they can't afford it! – so everyone agrees to blow off the concert and to spend Ross's birthday together instead.

Hurray! But wait…

The rich friends try to make amends by buying the poor friends the concert tickets – this seems like charity and is roundly rejected. The rich friends, angry that their gesture was rebuffed, attend the concert anyway, while the poor friends stay at home. The next day, the rich friends tell the poor friends that the concert was rubbish, everyone agrees not to let something as stupid as money affect their friendship, the poor friends discover that the rich friends lied – their night out was actually incredible – a huge row breaks out and then Monica is fired.

Phew! Now, let's get into it.

Best Animal Appearances

Sometimes you just need someone (something) to rest their head on your lap, stare at you adoringly and listen to all your woes non-stop with no interruptions. If human-friends aren't willing to do this (selfish), that's the time for animal-pals to shine. Over the course of the show, the gang were often upstaged by their furry (or decidedly un-furry) co-stars. Here we rank the appearances by animals that made big impressions, be they two- or four-legged, illegal, plastic or totally imaginary.

12. Pat, the giant ceramic dog
When Monica tells the removal men in the finale, 'If that [Pat] falls off the truck, it wouldn't be the worst thing', it signals the end of an extraordinary eight-season run for the giant ceramic dog. Pat's most iconic moment though is undoubtedly Chandler and Joey triumphantly riding him into Monica and Rachel's 'old' apartment (4.12).

SIDE NOTE: Pat actually belonged to Jennifer Aniston who was given him as a good-luck gift when starting the show.

11. Mitzi the hamster
Ross's date, beautiful doctoral candidate Cheryl (Rebecca Romijn), lives in a scene from Monica's nightmares (genuinely – the end credits show her turning up with cleaning supplies because it's keeping her up at night). When Ross kills something moving in a bag of snacks,

Cheryl screams: "Stop! It's my hamster – it's Mitzi!" Luckily it's not Mitzi though – it's just a rat (4.06).

10. Mozzarella (the happiest dog in the world)

Phoebe lends her friend's pet, Mozzarella, 'the happiest dog in the world', to Joey who's depressed about his feelings for Rachel. After pouring his heart out to the bouncy dog, Mozzarella is so sad he has to be taken back home (8.15).

9. Clunkers

Phoebe's dog-sitting escapade with shaggy Clunkers while she's staying at Monica and Chandler's apartment leads to one of the most traumatic and unforgivable discoveries within the group: Chandler hates dogs (7.08).

8. Paolo's cat

Ross is just about to reveal his feelings to Rachel for the first time while they're both out on the balcony star-gazing in Season 1…when a cat leaps on his back. The ensuing struggle seen through the apartment window is not only hilarious but leads to the introduction of the cat's owner: crapweasel Paolo (1.07).

7. Chick and Duck Jr.

Joey buys Chick and Duck Jr. as moving-away gifts for Chandler and Monica. The fact they then get stuck in the foosball table, which has to be dismantled is a poignant symbolic gesture that while situations change and foosball tables die, friendships last forever (10.17, Part 2).

6. Chappy
Ross is chuffed to bits that he's going to escort Chappy, Mike's family dog, down the aisle during Phoebe and Mike's wedding. It means he, unlike Chandler, is part of the ceremony (10.12). Turns out though that Chappy stinks – and Chandler ends up getting to walk the bride down the aisle instead. Sucks to be you, Ross.

5. Mrs Whiskerson (the hairless cat)
Thank God that Rachel is able to sell Mrs Whiskerson, a rare Sphynx cat, for a tidy profit to hapless Gunther. No one wants that hairless monstrosity in their apartment, even if it does remind her of a cat her grandmother used to have (5.21).

4. Phoebe's mum-cat/Julio
Ross saying sorry to 'Mrs Buffay' (Julio the cat), after aggressively telling Phoebe the spirit of her dead mum definitely doesn't reside in a random cat found on the street, is one of the best-worst moments in the show. Well done Rachel for suggesting the cat would appreciate the gesture (4.02).

3. The chick and the duck

Sure, they're adorable and provide many of Chandler and Joey's best coupledom moments, but, let's be honest, the chick and the duck are the source of so many unanswered questions. How isn't Chandler and Joey's apartment filled with bird crap – are the birds toilet-trained? How doesn't Treeger, the building superintendent, find out? Where do they suddenly disappear to in Season 6? Why do we only find out they died (shh...don't tell Joey) in the finale?

2. Marcel

Ross's substitute wife, capuchin monkey Marcel, is one of the most surreal storylines in the show. The one-sidedness of the relationship, the fact Marcel is horrible, and that keeping him is entirely illegal – it's all top-quality content, but Marcel's real moment of glory was getting the entire gang to sing 'The Lion Sleeps Tonight', complete with head-bobbing (2.12, Part 1).

1. Smelly Cat

Phoebe's song about a funky-smelling feline is arguably as famous as the show's theme tune. Taking on a life of its own outside the show, 'Phoebe' even performed Smelly Cat with *Friends* superfan Taylor Swift during the star's '1989' world tour in 2015. And yes, before you ask, she did give Swift pointers (mid-song) on the correct way to perform the track.

WHERE THE EPISODE WENT WENT WRONG

Everything! Firstly, Chandler putting on a birthday 'hoopla' for Ross without clearing it with everyone else beforehand is myopic. That he then doubles down by justifying the expense with 'But…it's Ross' is emotionally manipulative, even if unintentionally so. It correlates expense with Ross's worth as a friend. You could say 'But…it's Monica/Rachel/Chandler/Joey/Phoebe', it doesn't matter — the fact you can't afford a fancy-pants gift for your friend does not in any way infer the value you place on them as a person. To suggest otherwise is terrible.

Things then take a turn for the worse at dinner, because, despite Chandler encouraging the others to discuss what's on their minds, this genuinely important conversation gets waylaid by Ross's discovery and excitement about the Hootie concert… and then disappointment that they now may not go. It turns into a discussion about one specific event rather than an acknowledgement that this is an ongoing issue. That's why when Monica, Chandler and Ross comp the concert tickets for the others, they're furious. If you've just told your friends that you don't think they respect the truth of your financial situation and their answer is to essentially buy their way out of it, you'd be forgiven for feeling miffed at this 'charity' too. However, the poor friends definitely don't have to respond as aggressively as they do. Making anyone feel small was clearly not the intention behind the gesture. Also, how were the rich friends meant to know how strongly the poor friends felt about it when they kept playing it down, saying everyone should forget it, it doesn't matter, it's uncomfortable and let's not talk about it?

That the rich friends go to the concert and have a great time is fine. That they lie and say the evening was terrible, isn't. Then, when caught out in this lie, the fact Chandler justifies it by saying, 'I'm sorry that we make more money than you, but we're not going to feel guilty about it. We work really hard for it' is decidedly not okay. It sucks on two different levels:

1. **There's the inference that by bringing up the subject at all the poor friends have made the rich friends feel guilty.**

2. **It's also equating how hard someone works with how much money they have, which is ludicrous and insulting.**

Chandler doesn't mean either of these things. He's a kind and sensitive person who cares about his friends. These are classic knee-jerk defensive responses to this kind of uncomfortable conversation and it's great that the series addresses that. Much of what is said in this episode taps into the deep fears people have over money that stop them from speaking up about these issues in the first place. Which is why it's such a huge letdown that the show doesn't then analyse these back and forths and reassure viewers that things could have gone much better. That horrible line from Chandler is never dissected or shown to be untrue, it's just left hanging in the air as almost immediately afterwards Monica is fired.

Essentially, the series shows the worst-case scenario of a genuinely difficult conversation…and offers no resolutions. It only concludes by 'reassuring' everyone that being bumped from the rich side of the table to the poor side is just a phone call away.

Cheers for that.

WHAT SHOULD HAVE HAPPENED

All of this – absolutely all of it – could have been avoided HAD THEY SPOKEN TO EACH OTHER OPENLY AND HONESTLY. It's all about communication. Neither the poor friends nor the rich friends are mind-readers, yet each side starts resenting the other for what they see as insensitivity. How is either side meant to know what's happening with the other if no one says anything? If the poor friends keep chipping in for gifts they can't afford and going to 'nice' restaurants, the rich friends will think it's fine. Sure, you'd like to imagine they'd twig that a waitress, masseuse and jobbing actor won't earn as much as a paleontologist, head chef and 'transponster', but some people don't think about these things. So TELL THEM. If you don't, you're enabling their behaviour. Here are a couple of common examples of this:

- You constantly loan your friend money and comp their nights out until it becomes expected and then start resenting the assumption that you'll pay.
- You're asked to contribute a huge sum to a bachelor or bachelorette party and resentfully pay up but are grumpy every minute of the event.

When Chandler first mentions the $62, the poor friends could have said, 'I'm really sorry, I can't afford that right now. I can do X and Y, but not Z.' When it's suggested that they go to a nice restaurant, they could suggest an alternative: 'How about this really cool (cheaper) place down the road? It's all I can afford right now', 'How about I cook?' or 'How about I meet you for drinks afterwards?' If they do end up at the 'nice' restaurant though, they could have said at the start, 'This is a bit pricey, is it cool that we don't split the bill? I can only afford a few things.' If the bill is still being split and they feel bad about it, instead of snapping at the others, they could say: 'I'm sorry, I didn't realize we'd be splitting it. I can only afford to pay for what I had.' They also shouldn't minimize their own feelings or the situation by dismissing it as stupid — it's not. Money is a huge issue within friendship groups, especially when one or two people start to do better than the others.

As far as the rich friends go: they should listen! Their friends are trying to reveal something important and difficult. The default response should not be defensiveness about their privilege. The poor friends aren't saying the rich can't spend their money however they choose. They're simply asking that they be more aware that they may not be able to join in with everything and that compromises will need to be made when they are all hanging out together. This involves discussing the logistics of events before booking them to avoid any potential awkwardness in the future.

What could be more reasonable than that?

Chandler Muriel Bing

NICKNAMES/ALIASES: Mr. Big; Bing-a-Ling; Ms Chanandler Bong; Duck; Toby; Bing; Chan-Chan Man; The Boy Who Hates Thanksgiving; Smokey Joe.

PARENTS: Charles Bing/Helena Handbasket and Nora Tyler Bing.

SIBLINGS: Chandler is an only child.

RELATIONSHIP: Notable mentions for Janice and Kathy, but of course, Monica is the love of his life.

CHILDREN: Jack and Erica Bing (adopted with Monica in Season 10).

HISTORY WITH THE FRIENDS: Best friends with then roommate Ross since freshman year in college. Met Monica (and Rachel) for the first time when joining Ross for his family's Thanksgiving dinner. His history with Rachel is one of the few inconsistencies in the show (see page 24).

CHILDHOOD: Scarred by learning of his parents' divorce during Thanksgiving as a child (and that they had both slept with the pool boy), he refuses to celebrate the family holiday. His parents' acrimonious split, his father's Vegas drag show and his mother's flirtatiousness all led to him developing his sarcastic sense of humour as a defence mechanism.

PROFESSION: Statistical analysis and data reconfiguration (transponster); junior advertising copywriter.

KEY FLASHBACK MOMENT: When he and Ross reveal they've formed a college band called 'Way, No Way' (10.11); when Monica overhears him calling her fat (5.08); and when he kisses Rachel at a college party (10.11).

PERSONALITY: Quick-witted, innovative, encouraging and ridiculously self-deprecating. Intuitive, he's great at knowing when things aren't right with his friends. He appreciates creativity and bravery in others, has low self-esteem and deals with awkward situations by being sarcastic, even if it's really not a good time. A great lunch date and an excellent hugger.

MEMORABLE QUOTE: 'Dear God – this parachute is a knapsack!'

INTERESTING FACT: Matthew Perry has revealed that his favourite ever quip from the show was when Chandler told Joey: 'You have to stop the Q-tip when there's resistance.' (2.01).

CHECK YOURSELF AND RECOGNIZE YOU DON'T KNOW THE FULL STORY

Many money-related issues can be linked back to the 'Don't Take Things Personally' section in Chapter 3 (see page 66) and also the fact that you never know the full story. While you may think everyone will enjoy splashing out on a bachelorette party, that may not be a priority for your friends. Or, while you think it's bad form that your friend is buying a hairless cat even though she owes you money, maybe there's something deeper going on. Before you furiously demand answers, check in with your own emotions: are you shocked, angry, hurt or insecure? This kind of self-assessment is a much healthier basis on which to start a conversation as it'll be more honest and considerate. We often jump to conclusions or project our own experiences on to everyone else, with horrible results, as Ross discovers when he forces Joey to confront his Visa bill in 'The One Where Eddie Won't Go'. He projects his own fears around financial security on to Joey, ordering him to take a job he doesn't want in order to settle his debts. Joey tells him 'You're supposed to be my friend…tell me things like "Joey, you'll be fine"'. In the end Ross apologizes, acknowledging that he projected his own fears and reacted in a knee-jerk way (panic!). A kinder, more considered response would have gone a long way.

No matter how well we know our friends, we're not granted access to their innermost thoughts. And, knowing how difficult people find discussing money, chances are they're likely to be more secretive and even downright weird about their finances than almost any other topic. Don't ever assume you know everything. Sure, your friend may get paid hundreds of thousands of pounds at his high-flying job, but maybe he's also paying off a gambling debt you don't know about. Perhaps your friend who minutely splits the bill down to the last penny isn't just a monstrous pain in the ass but has had to suddenly take on all her mum's bills too. And maybe your friend who owes you money bought the hairless cat because she's lonely.

YOU CAN SAY 'NO'

There's an old saying: 'Before borrowing money from a friend, decide which you need most.' One thing *Friends* does cover extensively is both borrowing and lending money. There's a brilliant scene in Season 8 when Joey, in a rage that Chandler falls asleep during the premiere of his film, decides he wants to clear his debt to his friend after years of borrowing money for everything from headshots and dialect classes to tap-dancing lessons and food. After doing some calculations though, he realizes it comes to such an eye-watering sum that he immediately forgives Chandler for falling asleep and laughs it off.

Joey's borrowing is never really addressed as a serious issue – indeed, Chandler is so generous he invents the game 'Cups' in order to give him money without it seeming like a handout. With the others, we discover Monica has previously lent Rachel money after we meet the 'cat' and Phoebe lends Monica money to get her catering business off the ground. Both of these situations turn awkward. When Phoebe asks for her money back super-quickly, Monica is taken totally unawares, and when she in turn addresses the cat situation, Rachel ignores it. The lesson here is that if you're going to enter into this kind of agreement with friends, there have to be clear boundaries set from the off to avoid any misunderstandings or resentments. Phoebe should have specified when she needed the money back and Monica should have set up a plan with Rachel. One thing's clear though: if there is a plan in place, what your friend chooses to do with the money is none of your business. Unless they default on your agreement, you have to keep your opinions to yourself. Therefore, if you know you'll be internally fuming and judging every purchase they make with 'your' money, don't lend it to them. It's okay to say no because no one wants to get into a Richard Dreyfuss situation.

LESSONS LEARNED

- Money matters. Sure, conversations about cash are uncomfortable, but they're necessary – otherwise you'll get into situations that everyone feels defensive about.

- You can say no to borrowing or lending cash if it will make you edgy. Just be honest about it.

- Remember, you may not know the full story if your friend's behaving badly or strangely with cash. Don't project or assume, just ask.

CHAPTER 6

THE ONE WITH
THE ARGUMENTS

'It's always better to lie than to have the complicated discussion.'

Chandler, 'The One With Rachel's Phone Number' (9.09)

The bickering and arguments in *Friends* are part of what makes the show so relatable. Our pals drive us mad. The more time we spend with them, the more their foibles and tics and idiosyncrasies can get under our skin. And then there's the times they don't abide by The Code (see page 71) and all hell breaks loose. Or at least it does in your head while you um and ahh over saying anything because you don't like confrontation.

One of the biggest and most important arguments in *Friends* – and one of the best-remembered storylines in general –

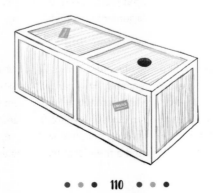

is when Chandler kisses Kathy, Joey's girlfriend (4.07). This betrayal leads to one of the most serious friendship breakdowns on the show. Chandler not only violates The Code but lies about it. It's a genuinely heart-wrenching moment because we can see both sides: how it happened (he and Kathy were made for each other!) and also how hurt Joey is. We can put ourselves in both of their shoes.

The same goes with Rachel and Ross's 'We were on a break!' storyline. To this day, fans still debate whose side they're on. Was Ross sleeping with Chloe (aka the 'hot girl from the Xerox place') understandable because he and Rachel were technically on a break? Or was his behaviour unforgivably pond-scummy regardless? Like the Joey and Chandler storyline, the reason this hits such a nerve is because most of us will recognize the horror of the situation. Unless you're an angel or a hermit, chances are you'll have made some questionable decisions, ones fuelled by jealousy, insecurity or because you fancy someone you shouldn't. You may not have slept with a hot Xerox girl the same night you had a row with your partner or kissed your best friend's significant other, but none of us can claim to be squeaky clean. And, equally likely is that you've also been the victim in these kinds of scenarios too: betrayed by someone you love. That's what the series does so well: presents both sides of an argument in a relatable way, including the fallout.

Above all, what the show clarifies for viewers is that arguments are an inevitable part of friendship. How can people who meekly agree to avoid all disagreements – brush them under the rug and pretend they don't exist – ever reach a deep connection? It's not about making a drama over nothing (there's no quicker way to end a friendship than constantly doing that) but about agreeing to hear each other out. Making a commitment to face something difficult together is saying you're in this for the long haul because you'd only ever bother arguing about proper stuff with someone you care about. Having a row means getting to know each other better, learning what upsets you both, what lines you can't cross and clearing up misunderstandings that otherwise would fester and change your opinion of each other. Arguing shows you trust and respect one another enough to be vulnerable.

Key lessons can be learned from the best and worst ways the gang thrash things out and by recognizing some of the biggest triggers of their dramas.

THE GANG'S MAIN TACTIC FOR DEALING WITH ISSUES: AVOIDANCE

Every character avoids discussing complicated or upsetting things on a daily basis. Indeed, avoidance is one of the founding actions upon which a lot of the show's comedy is based. Here's a small selection of examples:

- Phoebe doesn't tell Monica she's moved out. (3.06)
- Ross doesn't tell Rachel they're still married. (6.03)
- Chandler doesn't tell Joey he has feelings for Kathy. (Season 4)
- Ross and Rachel don't tell each other how they feel. (Every season)
- Chandler and Joey don't say they want to move back in together. (Season 2)

- Chandler doesn't tell Joey he dislikes the bracelet Joey's gifted him. (2.14)

- Rachel doesn't admit she always exchanges presents. (Every season)

- Rachel doesn't admit she lost Monica's earring. (5.19)

The show does a great job in proving that avoidance always makes things worse. Yes, pretending an issue doesn't exist, stewing on it privately or catastrophizing the fallout make for great comedy moments, but only because the end result is so much worse than it would have been had they just dealt with the original issue straight away. Guilt-ridden Chandler has to endure weeks of pretending not to be in love with Kathy, tormented at having to see her wander around the apartment wearing only a T-shirt. He also has to deal with hiding something of that magnitude from Joey, the very person he'd usually confide in. Joey, of course, realizes something's going on, but doesn't know what and so starts feeling confused and upset. Then there's Phoebe who, as a result of avoidance,

Ross Eustace Geller

NICKNAMES/ALIASES: Ross the Divorcer; Divorce-o; The Divorce Force; Professor McNails-His-Students; Mother Kisser; Cookie Duuuude; The Dinosaur Guy; Bea; Falafel Guy.

PARENTS: Jack and Judy Geller.

SIBLINGS: Monica Geller.

NOTABLE RELATIONSHIPS: Carol (ex-wife); Julie; Bonnie; Emily (ex-wife); Charlie; Rachel (ex-wife).

CHILDREN: Ben Geller (mother: Carol); Emma Geller-Green (mother: Rachel).

HISTORY WITH THE FRIENDS: As Monica's older brother, he knows her best school friend Rachel from when they were kids. He meets Chandler at college.

CHILDHOOD: Grew up as the favourite child of Jack and Judy Geller on Long Island, New York. The family is Jewish, as stated in 'The One With the Holiday Armadillo' (7.10). Has a fiercely competitive but very close relationship with sister Monica and he's very protective of her.

PROFESSION: Paleontologist; College Professor.

KEY FLASHBACK MOMENT: In 'The One With the Prom Video' (2.14), the group watch an old home movie that shows a moustachioed Ross quickly putting on a tux to take a distraught Rachel to prom after she's stood up by her date, Chip. Seeing Ross's face when he comes downstairs to find that Chip's turned up after all prompts Rachel to forgive Ross for his pros and cons list about her.

PERSONALITY: Ross is introverted, finding fulfilment in intellectual pursuits for which he was always praised as a child. Detail- and fact-oriented, he has a need to always be right and for people to agree with him (like arguing with Phoebe over evolution and the fact a cat can't be the reincarnated spirit of her mother). He's organized, controlling, competitive, paranoid, jealous and arrogant, but also very sweet, caring and loyal to his friends. He wants to do what's best even if it hurts him (like agreeing Joey can date Rachel even though it drives him mad).

MEMORABLE QUOTE: 'PIVOT!'

INTERESTING FACT: Ross and Rachel's relationship wasn't meant to be the central romance of the series – Monica and Joey's was. (Whaaaat?). However, the focus was changed after discovering the natural chemistry between David Schwimmer and Jennifer Aniston during initial read-throughs.

pretends she still lives in Monica's apartment! She arrives before Monica wakes up every morning and even pretends to go to bed in her old room. All to avoid having a conversation they end up having anyway…which turns out fine.

But the avoidance pièce de résistance has to be Ross evading the annulment of his Vegas marriage to Rachel – and then avoiding admitting it too. Rachel is so livid upon finding out that she storms into the auditorium where he's delivering a lecture to confront him. She then retaliates by claiming he's a gay intravenous drug user in the court papers, which ensures the annulment is chucked out by an unimpressed judge.

By putting something off, you're not giving yourself the chance to disprove your negative beliefs. You assume the worst will happen, playing out the scene in your head like a movie, and experience all of the negative emotions and thoughts associated with that result. These thoughts then snowball until dealing with it seems impossible. However, in reality, your worst-case scenario is never usually realistic and even if the absolute worst *does* happen, you can cope with it better than you think.

In Chandler's case, when he finally fesses up to Joey about his feelings, Joey's fine with it – he even gives them his blessing. His reaction is totally the opposite to Chandler's worst fears – Chandler's been winding himself up over nothing for weeks. However, because he avoided the issue he's now made everything a million times worse by a) kissing Kathy and b) lying about it.

When Phoebe finally does tell Monica she's moved out, her friend is more upset by the fact she hid it from her than by the actual issue. Even so, the conversation still ends with a big hug and 'I love yous'. That's the confrontation Phoebe was avoiding? Sheesh. Sign us up for some of that.

The lesson is clear: avoidance only aggravates stress and anxiety over an issue. You're now not only worried about the original problem, but also your avoidance of it. The worst-case scenarios you're convinced are real, aren't. They're anxiety-driven thoughts made up by your stressed-out brain. When considering avoiding something, ask yourself, 'What's *realistically* the worst that might happen? Can I cope with that? Have I ever dealt with something like this before? Do I trust my friend to want to work this out? What advice would I give to another friend dealing with this situation?' (The last question is important as we're always kinder to other people than to ourselves.) You'll be surprised by how manageable most problems become when looking at them objectively. Imagine the anxiety and stress you'll save yourself by facing it head-on. Then you can consider your options in dealing with it: make a plan, ask for advice, apologize or forgive.

THE *FRIENDS'* OTHER METHOD: OUTRIGHT LIE

The group lie to each other all the time. It's just as Chandler says in the opening quote to this chapter: 'It's always better to lie than to have the complicated discussion.' I mean, let's not be worthy about this: the man's right up to a point. If you have someone's best interests at heart (no, not your own), lying can be a benevolent thing to do. Telling your friend (Joey) that the musical theatre production they're appearing in as singing psychologist Freud is the worst play you've ever seen

(1.06) would only hurt their feelings. The gang know this and have tactics for getting out of telling the whole truth: 'Hey! You're in a play! I didn't know you could dance! You had a beard!'

A couple of other examples of 'good' lying:

- **When the gang pretends to love Rachel's meat trifle. (6.09)**
- **That they all think Phoebe's singing and Ross's keyboard-playing are great.**
- **Chandler saying how much he loves Monica's massages. (5.13)**

In all of those situations, lying is understandable. No one is getting hurt or betrayed by the lie and telling the truth wouldn't dramatically improve anyone's wellbeing (except perhaps that of Chandler's shoulders). However, lying turns bad when it's solely and consciously undertaken to save your own skin and make your own life easier. Like with avoidance, this 'solution' often becomes more damaging than the original problem. Take what happens between Chandler and Joey in 'The One With Ross's Grant' (10.06) when Chandler lies by telling Joey he watched his audition tape and passed it on to the casting director at his advertising agency. Joey is incensed because he knows Chandler's lying and Chandler is incensed at being called a liar ('But you are a liar,'

Rachel tells him, confused). Joey says he can prove Chandler's lying – and then quite spectacularly does so, playing the first clip on the tape: a Japanese advert featuring Joey wearing bright blue lipstick. He knows there's absolutely no way Chandler would have seen that and not laughed at him for decades.

When Chandler apologizes for not passing on the tape, Joey makes sure he knows that's not even the main problem anymore: 'That's not the point, Chandler. The point is that you lied.' Chandler acknowledges this and asks what it's going to take to be forgiven – cut to a scene of Chandler in the coffee house wearing blue 'Ichiban!' lipstick.

> **JOEY: First you lied, right? Then you lied about lying, okay? Then you lied about lying about lying, okay? So before you lie about lying about lying about lying…STOP LYING!**

Lying to friends is a tricky business, but no one can claim total ignorance as to what constitutes a 'good' or 'bad' lie. We all know when we're lying to avoid a tricky, but important conversation. Like when Ross lies to Rachel about reading her 18-page letter ('Front and back!'). He can pretend to everyone all he likes that he's doing it to protect her feelings, but everyone knows he's actually just protecting himself from having to admit he fell asleep and from having to deal with her disappointment.

Chandler is wrong: lying is only okay when it's selfless, not selfish. It should never be used as a tactic for getting out of inevitable and necessary conversations.

How Not to be Confrontational

- Wait until you're both calm enough to talk. Chandler lets Joey storm into his bedroom after Joey discovers his lie about watching the audition tape. Sometimes both of you need to cool down before a rational conversation is possible.

- Don't speak about the issue behind the person's back with other friends. Finding out about that is often more problematic than the original issue (aka when Ross tells Rachel that Monica agrees they were on a break).

- Try to stay super calm even if they're raising their voice (like everyone does with both Phoebe and Rachel when they're at the end of their pregnancies, and as they do with Ross during his super-angry phase in Season 5).

- Definitely don't resort to petty insults, giving the finger or banging your fists together in Ross's version of flipping the bird (unless they really deserve it).

ANOTHER COMMON ARGUMENT STARTER: THINKING YOU'RE A MIND-READER

In 'The One With the Ring' (6.23), viewers see a classic set-up for arguments: when you presume to know why someone is behaving a certain way and then react to that assumption. The vicious circle below shows how this can escalate:

Joey and Ross are so convinced they know why Chandler is being distant they actually get offended by a reason they've completely invented. We do this all the time — believe we're mind-readers and then act on what we think we know. Right now, you're probably mad at someone or upset over something

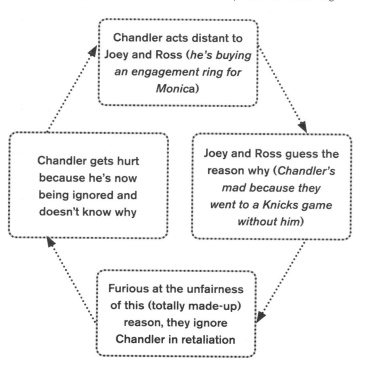

Chandler acts distant to Joey and Ross (*he's buying an engagement ring for Monica*)

Joey and Ross guess the reason why (*Chandler's mad because they went to a Knicks game without him*)

Furious at the unfairness of this (totally made-up) reason, they ignore Chandler in retaliation

Chandler gets hurt because he's now being ignored and doesn't know why

The Best Ever Insults

Being able to wittily insult your friends without fear of seriously hurting their feelings is one of the clearest signs that your relationship is close. Good pals can say the unsayable. If a stranger called Ross out on having three ex-wives or Joey on sleeping around they would be (rightly) ex-communicated. But when the gang do it, it's hilarious. Here are some of the best put-downs from the show.

ROSS: Hello? Didn't you read *Lord of the Rings* in high school?

JOEY: No, I had sex in high school.

The One Where They're Gonna PARTY! (4.09)

The One Where No One's Ready (3.02)

RACHEL: Does this look like something the girlfriend of a paleontologist would wear?

PHOEBE: I don't know. You might be the first one.

ROSS: I went to that tanning place your wife suggested.

CHANDLER: Was that place… *the sun*?

The One With Ross's Tan (10.03)

MONICA: Why is your family Scottish?

CHANDLER: Why is your family Ross?

The One With Joey's New Brain (7.15)

RACHEL: I don't go for guys right after they get divorced.

MONICA: Right. You only go for them five minutes before they get married.

The One Where Ross Moves In (5.07)

JOEY: Yeah, it's never taken me more than a week to get over a relationship.

The One Without the Ski Trip (3.17)

MONICA: It's never taken you more than a shower to get over a relationship.

Judge the Line

Subjects the gang mock mercilessly include: Ross's divorce record and being a nerd, Chandler's manner of speaking, Monica's clean-freakishness, Phoebe's terrible boyfriend choices and mad upbringing, Joey being a bit slow on the uptake and sleeping around, and Rachel being spoiled. However, there are some topics that even they can't joke about, knowing that it will cross a line: infertility and heartbreak spring to mind. Being a good friend is knowing what you can get away with…and knowing when you've gone too far.

The One With Rachel's Other Sister (9.08)

ROSS: A PhD is just as good as an MD!

RACHEL: Oh, sure, Ross, yeah. If I have a heart attack in a restaurant, I want you there with your fossil brush.

The One With the Proposal (6.24)

CHANDLER (TO ROSS): I mean, if you're not careful, you may not get married at all this year.

you think you know: a reason you've projected on to a situation that you haven't actually verified. And, chances are, you're way off base. When we feel insecure, low or anxious, we're more likely to default to explanations that make things our fault: 'They're mad at me', 'They don't like me', 'I did something wrong'. We then behave in negative ways in response to these thoughts, by say, ignoring the person, being snappy with them or distancing ourselves. However, if we're feeling confident, secure and positive, we're more likely to be realistic about the cause for someone's behaviour: 'They must be busy', 'This likely has nothing to do with me', 'I've no idea why they did that – I'll ask'. You're not a mind-reader. Before you respond to something in ways that will escalate a situation, make sure you have all the facts.

SWALLOW THAT PRIDE: APOLOGIZE AND FORGIVE

We're all petty and mean sometimes. Yes, even you. And we all make mistakes. We're often more petty and mean to our super-close friends because we know they'll let us get away with it. Part of the beauty of that kind of closeness is being able to push the boundaries when it comes to jokes, honesty, being an ass and tough love. However, the secret to long-lasting friendships is knowing where that line is…and if you cross it, to suck it up, own up and admit that you're sorry. People just want to feel appreciated, loved and understood. If that means you have to eat humble pie, eat it and GET IN THE BOX, CHANDLER.

All the characters on the show are really good at apologizing when they need to (and sometimes when they don't) – and we can learn a lot from that. Here are a few examples of excellent sorries:

- **Rachel to Joey when she turns into her terrifying dad while teaching him to sail. (7.03)**
- **Monica when she asks Phoebe not to sing outside her posh restaurant. (9.19)**
- **Ross to Phoebe when he bullies her about evolution and her mum-cat. (2.03, 4.02)**
- **Joey to Ross after he proposes to Rachel. (9.02)**
- **Phoebe to Ross when she admits she mugged him as a teenager. (9.15)**

Saying sorry even if you don't think you're in the wrong can be the only option with stubborn pals. Rachel's great at this, often being the first to apologize after a row to clear the air. When she, Monica and Phoebe end up in a big fight over the (fictional) feminist book 'Be Your Own Windkeeper' (2.19), she's the first to step up and make things right by buying the others cake in the coffee shop. (She ends up taking the cake back so her waitress wages aren't docked, but it's the thought that counts.) Apologizing doesn't mean backing down on your principles or pretending you're not hurt, but if it's a simple case of everyone just wanting to be right, taking the higher road by swallowing your pride feels good.

Equally, if you need to accept an apology, do it. Ask yourself: is this worth losing my friend forever over? What will I gain from holding a grudge? Channel your inner Joey and Phoebe (who are excellent at accepting apologies), take them at their word and move on.

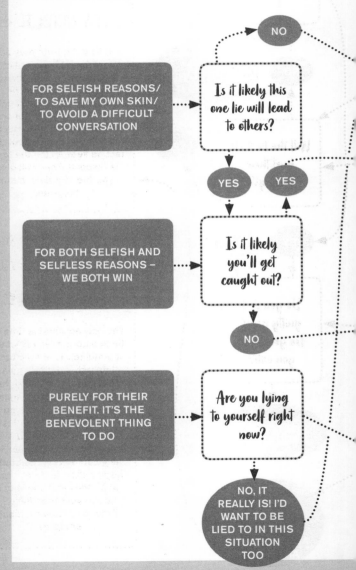

SHOULD YOU LIE OR TELL THE TRUTH TO YOUR FRIEND?

WHY ARE YOU CONSIDERING LYING TO A GOOD FRIEND?

FOR SELFISH REASONS/ TO SAVE MY OWN SKIN/ TO AVOID A DIFFICULT CONVERSATION

Is it likely this one lie will lead to others?

NO

YES

FOR BOTH SELFISH AND SELFLESS REASONS – WE BOTH WIN

Is it likely you'll get caught out?

YES

NO

PURELY FOR THEIR BENEFIT. IT'S THE BENEVOLENT THING TO DO

Are you lying to yourself right now?

NO, IT REALLY IS! I'D WANT TO BE LIED TO IN THIS SITUATION TOO

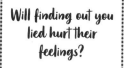
Will finding out you lied hurt their feelings?

NO

NO, THEY'LL UNDERSTAND WHY I DID IT

Will the lie itself hurt their feelings?

YES

YES

YES

Do you feel guilty now? Do you think you will?

NO, I FEEL OKAY ABOUT IT

SIGH. YES, OKAY. I'M JUST AVOIDING ADDRESSING AN ISSUE

IT'S TRUTH TIME

Telling the truth may be difficult, but it's a hell of a lot easier than being caught out in a lie. Think of Chandler and the lipstick audition tape – he not only had to deal with the fallout from the original lie, but the fact he lied! Telling the truth is respectful and will gain you friend-points in the long-run.

YOU CAN LIE...IF YOU KNOW THE CONSEQUENCES

The only acceptable time to lie to a good friend is when it genuinely is in their best interest and they'll gain nothing from knowing the truth: i.e. that their singing is dreadful (we're looking at you, Pheebs – haha! Just kidding! You're great!) The only other time you can lie is if you don't care about hurting their feelings – but what does that say about you or your friendship? Time for a reassessment sharpish.

Phoebe as (problematic) Peacemaker

In 'The One with the Ride Along' (5.20), Phoebe says: 'I'm a pacifist, but when the revolution comes, I'll destroy all of you. Except for you, Joey'. She's not lying. She doesn't shy away from a fight (maybe due to her time spent living on the street), but she also doesn't provoke them for no reason. She's actually very rational and straightforward, taking people at face-value and channelling a 'life's too short for petty squabbles' vibe. If she's annoyed, you'll know about it, but if you're annoyed she'll do her best to act as peacekeeper. This is why she threatens to throw the lottery tickets over the balcony in 9.18 (only for her peacekeeping plan to be foiled by a wayward pigeon who knocks the bowl out of her hands): 'If we're not doing this together, we're not doing it at all'. She even grabs the ears of Rachel and Monica during their fight over dating Jean-Claude Van Damme: 'If we were in prison, you guys would be, like, my bitches' (2.13). Her attempts to keep the peace may go wrong, but hey, at least she tries.

Having an argument about something important is healthy within close friendships. It means you trusted your bond enough to be vulnerable, let someone know how you feel and showed them it mattered. If you personally don't care enough to let someone know you're hurt, or, if you don't trust them enough to respond well, that's not a healthy friendship. Realizing someone's put their ego on the line and their feelings in your hands by revealing they're hurt, or by admitting they've hurt you, is a positive thing and you'll know each other better once you've come out the other side. You need to trust that the bonds you have with your friends can withstand these tests.

LESSONS LEARNED

- Avoiding or lying about an issue just aggravates the problem, adding guilt about that on top of everything else. Facing up to things will make you feel more in control.

- Friendship is about allowing yourself to be vulnerable: to tell people you're hurt or you did something wrong and to believe they'll care.

- Trust in your friendships: true bonds can withstand these tests and you'll come out stronger on the other side.

CHAPTER 7
THE ONE WHERE YOU HAVE EACH OTHER'S BACKS

'That's right I stepped up! She's my friend and she needed help! And if I had to, I'd pee on any one of you!'

Joey, 'The One With the Jellyfish' (4.01)

Being true friends means being able to rely on one another in the embarrassing, worrying, sad and even boring situations, as well as the fun, happy and exciting ones. It's about trusting that your pal will show up whether they want to or not, and whether they agree with you or not. Sure, different friends will be better suited to help with different circumstances, but you know whoever it is will drop everything to be with you when it really matters – and they know that you'll return the favour. Over 10 seasons and 236 episodes, Ross, Monica, Rachel, Phoebe, Chandler and Joey prove time and time again that the lyrics from the infamous theme tune are legit: they really will be there for each other when the rain starts to fall (sing along!).

Phoebe Buffay*

NICKNAMES/ALIASES: Regina Phalange; Princess Consuela Bananahammock; Ikea; Emma; Weird Girl; Valerie.

PARENTS: Lily Buffay (adopted mother), Phoebe Abbott (birth mother), Frank Buffay Sr. (father).

SIBLINGS: Ursula Buffay (twin sister), Frank Buffay Jr. (half-brother).

NOTABLE RELATIONSHIPS: Duncan Sullivan (ex-husband); David 'The Scientist Guy'; Mike Hannigan (husband).

CHILDREN: Carries triplets as a surrogate for her brother, Frank (a storyline included by the writers to successfully incorporate Lisa Kudrow's real life pregnancy).

HISTORY WITH THE FRIENDS: Monica's roommate before Rachel moves in.

CHILDHOOD: Ooof. Tough one. It's no wonder Rachel asks her, 'How have you never been on Oprah?' (2.09). Key facts: adoptive mother died by suicide; father abandoned her as a baby; stepdad went to prison (he used to sell his blood to buy her food); she lived on the street from 14-years-old; got hepatitis when a pimp spit in her mouth; was a mugger (and once mugged Ross); and she once stabbed a cop (but only because he stabbed her first).

PROFESSION: Massage therapist; waitress; TV extra; musician.

KEY FLASHBACK MOMENT: When she and Ross kiss in 'The One With The Flashback' (3.06). Phoebe and Ross! Wtf! They even roll around on the pool table and everything. It's the most unexpected hook-up scenario in the show's history.

PERSONALITY: Imaginative, original, optimistic, artistic, authentic, unconventional, weaves a great story, truthful and a free spirit. Not a people pleaser and doesn't care if people don't like her (as proven when she's entirely unbothered by Rachel's mum's anger when she and Monica forget her invite to Rachel's baby shower (8.20)). Has a tendency to put her foot in it and reveal secrets as well as dropping truth-bombs, but she's very useful at getting people out of boring parties (2.22).

MEMORABLE QUOTE: 'If you want to receive emails about my upcoming shows, please give me money so I can buy a computer.'

INTERESTING FACT: Ursula, Phoebe's twin sister, existed before Phoebe. Lisa Kudrow played Ursula, an absent-minded waitress, on 'Mad About You', the sitcom that ran back-to-back with *Friends* on NBC. Execs exploited the chance to create a kind of TV in-universe by making Phoebe Ursula's twin sister who would appear across both shows.

* Phoebe doesn't know her middle name. In 'The One Where They All Turn 30' (7.14) Phoebe discovers via her twin sister Ursula that not only are they actually 31 and not 30, but that Ursula sold Phoebe's birth certificate to a Swedish runaway and doesn't remember her sister's middle name.

And that's undoubtedly part of the show's longevity: we all aspire to both have and be friends like these.

Let's be honest though, it's not realistic to expect anyone to provide the same amount of support the friends in the show do. For starters, most people have jobs. When the rest of the gang muse over why all their bosses might hate them, Joey reckons he has a good idea: 'Maybe it's because you're all hanging around here at 11.30am on a Wednesday?' (6.08). Then there's the partners, family, pets, other friends and general life admin that all exert legitimate claims upon our time. We physically can't be at each other's beck and call 24/7. Expectations have to be pragmatic – but that's not licence to give less support, it just means having each other's backs in the best ways we can. It's possible to be supportive over DMs,

Genuine Friends for Life

How wonderful is it that the actors in the series genuinely seem to be such great friends in real life? Jennifer Aniston and Courteney Cox's regular Instagram posts of them just hanging out give us all the feels. As does the fact that in the years since the finale aired, the cast have never had anything but positive things to say about each other. This gives a kind of meta credence to their characters' friendships and an authenticity to the lessons we can take from the show.

Zoom, social media and, yes, by speaking on the phone (THE HORROR). Not many of us are lucky enough to live across the hall from our favourite people (if you are, well played), which means we have to work a little harder than the TV friends do, but we can still take inspiration from them in knowing how and when to step up.

YOU TURN UP EVEN WHEN YOU DON'T WANT TO

Whether it's turning up in person or in spirit, being a friend means showing support even if it's the last thing you feel like doing. Having each other's backs is easy when it involves going to a film premiere or to a conference in Barbados – it's balancing that stuff up with the decidedly less fun things that matter. Examples of when the friends nail this include:

- Peeing on your friend when they've been stung by a jellyfish. (Chandler for Monica – Joey tries but gets 'stage fright' (4.01))

- Becoming a vegetarian when your pregnant friend craves meat to 'even things out'. (Joey for Phoebe (4.16))

- Asking your friend to waitress for you even though she's the worst waitress that ever lived. (Monica for Rachel (1.15))

- Saying you'll give up your dream job as a head chef to honour the promise you made to co-found a catering company. (Monica for Phoebe (4.09))

- Telling your friend she doesn't have to give up her dream job as a head chef. (Phoebe for Monica (4.09))
- Teaching your friend how to talk dirty. (Joey for Ross (1.15))
- Kissing your friend to help him practise for an audition. (Ross for Joey (2.24))

The gang regularly sacrifice their time, pride, money and dignity (but not their meatball subs) in order to help the others out. They prioritize their friends and their friendships above their own wants and needs because they know it's reciprocal and because it feels damn good to be there for someone you love. Asking yourself, 'When have I done this recently?' is a good way to work out if you need to step up. It's also essential to learn to ask for help when you need it and not to feel like a burden. Asking your pals to help you carry a couch up three flights of stairs is par for the course for good friends (screaming 'PIVOT!' in their faces as they do it is negotiable). On the whole, people

like being asked for help or advice. It makes them feel valued. Like Phoebe, they can always say no ('I wish I could, but I don't want to'), but, your friends aren't mind-readers: unless you ask, they won't know what you need.

YOU ACCEPT EACH OTHER'S 'FLAWS', QUIRKS AND WEIRDNESSES

So one of your pals is convinced an old woman's soul is inhabiting her body (2.11) and another loses their mind when you say Jurassic Park could happen (4.02). Then there's the friend who flat out refuses to celebrate national holidays (1.09) and the siblings who'll spend 12 hours playing a mad version of American football for the glory of winning a 20-year-old Troll doll (3.09). Our friends' eccentricities are what make them unique and special. It would be incredibly boring if we only associated with people exactly the same as us. And here's news: you're weird too. No really, you are. We asked around.

A lot can be learned from how Ross and Phoebe deal with their fundamental differences: they simply don't engage (much) on those topics. Ross cannot deal with Phoebe's rejection of science, and Phoebe cannot deal with Ross's insistence that she has to adhere to his view. Their huge row on evolution notwithstanding (2.03), their general approach is to happily tease each other while avoiding getting too seriously into these topics as they know genuine problems would arise. Instead, they show support in other ways, such as Ross being super-excited about Phoebe's dollhouse and trying to put out the ensuing fire (3.20) and Phoebe driving Ross to the airport to try to stop Rachel getting on the plane in the finale.

The things that annoy us about our friends can often be what makes them great in other areas of their lives. For example, Monica's perfectionism is what makes her a fantastic chef; Joey's overt confidence is what makes him a brilliant actor (let's not argue over the 'brilliant', okay, let's just be supportive); and Chandler's readiness with a witty line is what makes him a perfect copywriter. It's not our place to see anything as a 'flaw', no matter our own views. They're not flaws, but facts about

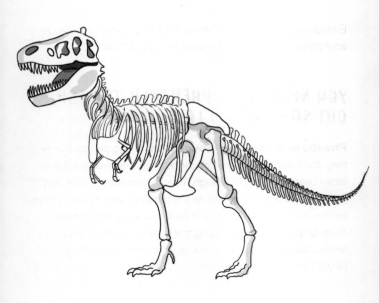

people we care about. This is why Ross's pros and cons list about Rachel hurts her so much: 'Imagine the worst things you think about yourself. Now, how would you feel if the one person that you trusted the most in the world not only thinks them too, but actually uses them as reasons not to be with you?' (2.08) This isn't a betrayal of Rachel as a potential romantic partner (where we're much less forgiving of things that would annoy us), but of her as a friend. Friends are meant to accept you no matter what, with no conditions attached, not suggest things they'd want to change about you in an ideal world. If they do see these things as deal-breakers then they're not good friends. Why should the fact your pal is slightly spoiled affect you on a daily basis if you don't let it? The guys may have advocated using pros and cons lists for dates before, but never for friends and that's where they cross a line.

Embracing the differences in our friends and knowing they've accepted ours too is what makes life rich and interesting.

YOU NEED TO BE PREPARED TO DISH OUT SOME TOUGH LOVE

Phoebe is the queen of tough love: telling people things they don't want to hear out of concern for their welfare. It's a tricky beast to get right though. Your motivation, the time and place you dish it out, as well as the temperament of the person on the receiving end all have to be taken into consideration. An example of Phoebe getting this spot-on is when she tries to stop Rachel flying to London to crash Ross's wedding (4.23, Part 1):

Chandler's Best Quips

Chandler uses his quick wit in lots of ways: to defuse tension, as a defence mechanism, as a means of self-deprecation, as a way of putting his friends in their place – and because he simply can't help himself. It's a great example of a character trait that's both a flaw and a strength – and it is a quirk that the group all embrace as a central part of what makes Chandler, Chandler. To celebrate that, here are some of the funniest gags from the King of the Quips.

The One With the Tiny T-shirt (3.19)

JOEY: Just because she went to Yale Drama she thinks she's, like, the greatest actress since, since…sliced bread!

CHANDLER: Ahh, sliced bread. A wonderful Lady Macbeth.

ROSS: I can't believe you two had sex in her dream.

CHANDLER: I'm sorry, it was a one-time thing. I was very drunk and it was someone else's subconscious.

The Pilot (1.01)

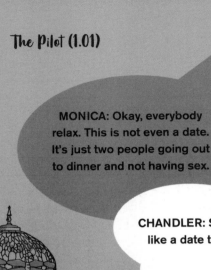

MONICA: Okay, everybody relax. This is not even a date. It's just two people going out to dinner and not having sex.

CHANDLER: Sounds like a date to me.

You do you

Chandler's inability to stop saying the first funny thing that comes to mind winds the group up non-stop. Ross even bets him $50 that he can't go a week without making fun of everyone (Chandler ends up paying Ross the $50 early because he's about to burst from withheld sarcasm (5.11)). However, just like Monica's perfectionism and shouty-ness, while the group are allowed to make fun of each other's quirks and find them annoying, outsiders aren't. That's why Joey dumps Janine after she says Chandler 'is blah' and Monica 'is very loud for such a small person' (6.11). The lesson being: to protect your friends' right to be themselves at all costs.

> PHOEBE: Look, Rachel, if you go, you're just going to mess with his head and ruin his wedding! Y'know, it's too late – you missed your chance. I'm sorry, I know this must be really hard, but it's over.

She's not only looking after Rachel's best interests here, but also Ross's. Her delivery is sympathetic and non-judgemental, acknowledging both the difficulty of the situation and Rachel's feelings, while also firmly explaining her reasons for believing it's a bad plan. Phoebe knows Rachel's intentions are selfish in that moment and she can only see things going awry.

For tough love to be effective, it needs to have the right intention behind it (i.e. to steer your friend away from a wrong decision) and be delivered in an appropriate way. In the previous episode to the one mentioned above, (4.22), there's a great example of tough love being dished out for all the wrong reasons.

When Rachel reveals she doesn't think she can attend the wedding, Phoebe says how that reminds her of the time she was living on the street and was solicited for sex in exchange for food. Confused, Rachel asks Phoebe how that's similar, to which Pheebs replies: 'Well, let's see, it's not really. Because, you see that was an actual problem, and uh, yours is just like, y'know, a bunch of high school crap that nobody really gives y'know…' This is just downright mean, with no redeeming motivation behind it. A meanness that is then topped off by Phoebe scowling, 'All right, here come the waterworks!' when Rachel cries. Phoebe's motivation here was solely to be snarky because she's nine months pregnant with her brother's triplets and bored, uncomfortable and grumpy.

Tough love also needs to be delivered sensitively in order to be effective rather than just cruel. When Phoebe believes a stray cat contains the spirit of her mum (4.02), none of the group are willing to broach the subject, even though they all agree it's necessary, except Ross, who exasperatedly shows Phoebe the 'Missing' poster a little girl has pasted all over town. Phoebe's response is to say Ross isn't being a good friend: 'I believe this is my mother. Even if I'm wrong, who cares? Just be a friend, okay? Be supportive.' And Ross actually ends up apologizing both to Phoebe and her mum-cat. Is this a case of Phoebe only being able to dish it out, not take it? Or, knowing Ross, is it more likely the self-righteousness of his delivery wound Phoebe up? We're firmly swaying towards the latter. Ross's motivations seem more driven by being right than by gently telling his friend that her behaviour isn't ideal. He's rude, judgemental and aggressive in his delivery. Had he been calmer and less intent simply on proving a point, Phoebe would no doubt have been more receptive.

True friends need to be prepared to shine a light on uncomfortable realities. If your friend's behaving badly, hurting other people, hurting themselves or in danger of looking like an ass, it's your job to tell them — because you'd want them to tell you, right? A good friend isn't someone who'll always tell you you're right, it's someone who'll tell you when you're wrong (with compassion), while reassuring you that they'll help deal with the fallout regardless. Tough love is a necessary part of friendship, just always make sure it's undertaken for the right reasons and in a kind and considerate way.

STANDING UP FOR THEM

When Joey storms into Rachel's boss's office and screams at him for wanting to 'buy my friend's baby' (8.17) it's a hilarious and beautiful example of standing up for a friend. Joey is good at this, even being willing to tell a friend off

(Monica) for upsetting another friend (Chandler): 'Did you tell Chandler that some guy from work is the funniest guy you ever met?…Really, do you not know Chandler?' (9.06) Defending our friends is a way of showing that we care – putting our money where our mouths are, as it were. It's all very well to talk a big game when it comes to supporting our pals, but to actually go out on a limb and make yourself uncomfortable shows you're willing to go that extra mile.

Some more examples of the crew putting themselves out there for each other include:

- **Phoebe defending Ross to the tenants in his new apartment building who think he's a cheapskate. (5.15)**
- **Ross sitting with Joey in the museum canteen. (4.11)**
- **Phoebe telling a casting director that Joey's attempts to speak French are the result of a childlike mental age. (10.13)**
- **The guys rushing upstairs to shout at their neighbour for sleeping with someone else the night after sleeping with Phoebe. (3.11)**
- **Rachel demanding Gunther give Joey his job back as a waiter. (6.12)**

There are also the times when you support people without them even knowing it, such as Ross letting Rachel win at poker (1.18) and Rachel chasing a pizza delivery girl down the street to ask her out for Ross (5.19). Of course it would always be easier not to get involved – not to stand up for someone or just to let things run their course – but that's not what friends are for.

'I'M NOT GREAT AT THE ADVICE. CAN I INTEREST YOU IN A SARCASTIC COMMENT?'

There are lots of ways to be supportive. You'll have friends you speak to nearly every day who would be useless in an emergency, but the best to laugh it off and hug it out with (Chandler). You'll have amazing friends that you can go months without speaking to, but who you know will be by your side immediately if you need them (Rachel and Ross). There are no fixed rules when it comes to having each other's backs – what individuals need and what you can expect in return is something learned through joint experience. Some of your friends may need more support than others, some may not be able to give as much as you'd like at points. It will ebb and flow, but through honesty and building a good foundation you can find your groove together. Supporting someone and being supported in return is liberating, reassuring and exciting. Life has a way of kicking us in the teeth when we least expect it, but that's okay – no, really it is. Why? Because you can handle anything when you have friends for life.

LESSONS LEARNED

- Telling the people you love home truths when necessary, and being told them in return, is a key part of friendship. Trust that you've all got each other's best interests at heart.

- We're all different so support people in different ways. Don't expect the same from everybody, but learn to ask for help when you need it.

- Our friends' eccentricities are what makes life interesting. Your pals should accept you and all your weirdnesses and you should return the favour.

THE ONE WITH THE TOP 10 FRIENDSHIP LESSONS WE LEARNED

1. Friendships take work

Taking your friends for granted spells trouble. Call them, invite them to Knicks games, like their Instagram posts, organize to see them (and don't cancel, even for sex, right Joey?). Ask yourself: 'Are my friendships balanced?' If not, put more work in or tell your friend you need them to step up (as Joey tells Chandler after Chandler moves in with Monica). Friends have no obligation to stick around, so make sure you're doing your bit.

2. Know when you've crossed the line

We all know we can push the boundaries with friends more than we can with other people, but there is a line – and everyone's lines are different. It's as Chandler says to Ross after he makes a joke about Chandler being unemployed: 'What are you doing? You know I can only dish it out!' (9.13). Be funny, but be kind, and always respect The Code.

3. Arguments can make friendships stronger

Telling your friend that you're hurt or admitting you've done something wrong is difficult but necessary for a stronger relationship. Dealing with the fallout takes courage, but is worth it (Joey understands how much he means to Chandler when Chandler proves he'd give up Kathy by staying silent in a box). We only have these kinds of discussions because we care. You'll learn more about your friend, you'll clear up all sorts of misunderstandings and you'll discover new things about each other that you can build on to make your connection deeper.

4. You can let go of bad friendships

Remember: friendships are relationships we choose – you don't have to put up with toxicity or spending time with people you're entirely ambivalent about (aka Amanda Buffamonteezi). You're not obligated, no matter the history or baggage you share. Don't ghost, but be honest, so you can extricate yourself knowing you've taken the higher ground and then forgive yourself – these things happen.

5. Lean on your friends and ask for help

Asking for help is a strength, not a weakness – and it's a two-way street. Asking your friends for help, showing you respect their opinions or that you need to lean on them will enable them to ask you in return. Whether it's helping them to move a couch up some impossible stairs ('PIVOT!'), to pretend you're pregnant so your mate can work out what she wants to do (cheers, Pheebs), or to sit in the back of their grandmother's cab while they argue with themselves about meeting their long-lost dad.

6. True friends will support you no matter what

Whether they're dishing out some tough love, feeding you ice cream after a break-up, attending the premiere of your latest terrible acting gig or sitting through your attempt at playing the bagpipes, true friends will be there for you no matter what. Even if they're not good at giving advice, but only at providing sarcastic comments, reassuring hugs and some laughs, that's friendship gold.

7. Your friends are your surrogate family

You probably spend more time with your friends than your family, they know you better, they protect you from your actual family and they're more fun to hang out with during emotionally fraught holidays (unless they make you play the Geller Cup). Your 'framily' stays close because they choose to, not because they have to – and that's powerful stuff.

8. You can be totally honest (and make fun of everyone)

Your friends know what's really going on, even if your 'real' family and social media followers have no idea. You can relentlessly mock them, but know when to stop and, best of all, when they ask if you'd like to help them build their Ikea furniture, with 'proper' friends you can say: 'I wish I could, but I don't want to', just like Phoebe.

9. You have to allow yourself to be vulnerable

True and deep connections are built upon vulnerability: allowing people in and letting them see you at your worst. It's about trust – knowing that they won't judge you or intentionally hurt you, but if they do, you'll work it out together. You know you can call them, whatever you've done and whenever you need a shoulder to cry on, confident that they have your best interests at heart (and that they'll share their 'good ice cream' with you).

10. Hugging it out really helps

The gang are excellent huggers. There isn't an episode that passes without someone providing a reassuring squeeze, shoulder grab or even a fist bump (this counts), to show they care. In these bizarre pandemic times we find ourselves living in, physical contact has become more important than ever. When your ability to hug whoever you want is taken away, you realize how much that physical connection matters. Make the most of it and hug, squeeze, hold hands or elbow bump whoever you love whenever you can.

REFERENCES,
FURTHER READING AND
ACKNOWLEDGEMENTS

REFERENCES AND FURTHER READING

- Saul Austerlitz: *Still Friends: 25 Years of the TV Show that Defined an Era* (Trapeze, 2019)
- http://www.gaytimes.co.uk/culture/friends-actress-kathleen-turner-says-show-hasnt-aged-well-lgbtq-rights-exclusive
- https://www.bbc.co.uk/news/entertainment-arts-42733705
- https://www.comedycentral.co.uk/
- https://friends.fandom.com/
- http://www.livesinabox.com/friends/
- https://en.wikipedia.org/wiki/Friends
- https://www.goodmorningamerica.com/culture/story/ways-knew-show-friends-influenced-tv-world-58898455
- https://www.nytimes.com/2019/09/05/arts/television/friends-tv-show.html
- https://hellogiggles.com/lifestyle/how-money-can-ruin-friendships/
- https://www.glamour.com/story/friends-episode-five-steaks-and-an-eggplant-money
- https://screenrant.com/myers-briggs-personality-types-friends-characters/
- https://www.bbc.com/culture/article/20190920-friends-the-show-that-changed-our-idea-of-family
- https://www.wellandgood.com/tough-love/

Useful websites

- Mood Gym: moodgym.anu.edu.au
- Relate: relate.org.uk
- The Mental Health Foundation: mentalhealth.org.uk
- The American Mental Health Foundation: americanmentalhealthfoundation.org
- Cruse Bereavement Care: cruse.org.uk
- Samaritans: samaritans.org
- Refuge: nationaldahelpline.org.uk
- MIND, The National Association for Mental Health: mind.org.uk

Acknowledgements

A huge thanks to Philippa Wilkinson, my brilliant editor at Quercus, for being receptive to every mad idea and to numerous iterations of 'Do you remember the one where…?' conversations. Thank you to Mel Elliot for creating such brilliant illustrations that bring to life all the friendship lessons in the book, and also to copyeditor Clare Hubbard for painstakingly checking every reference.

I'd also like to say a heartfelt and slightly apologetic thank you to my eternally patient partner Koen Laan, whose life was entirely taken over by the show for months (hey, could be worse – at least I wasn't writing a book on my other favourite subject: true crime). A big thanks also to those of my pals who are absolute *Friends* fanatics. Kate Lucey: my respect and admiration for your encyclopedic knowledge of the series knows no bounds. My 'Fringe Benefits' WhatsApp crew: thank you for always being up for a spontaneous quiz. Alex, Andy, Rosie and Sienna: I can't wait to see you soon.

One thing we didn't get a chance to really go into in the book was how to make new friends – a topic close to my heart after moving to the middle of nowhere in Holland recently. To those of you feeling lonely, I can recommend meetup.com, joining expat/interest groups on Facebook and using the Bumble app to 'date for friends'. I also asked existing friends to set me up on 'mate dates'. Thank you to everyone who did – you have nice pals! (And some shockers.)

Last, but obviously not least, the biggest thank you has to go to Marta Kauffman and David Crane, as well as all the actors who appeared, for creating such a timeless piece of televisual gold. Countless people have told me that they re-watched the show during lockdown, finding peace, comfort and laughter in its familiarity. I honestly think it's probably saved a few people from losing their minds. It's been a real privilege to write a book about something so universally beloved – it's made me realize all over again how genuinely unique and special it is. And the scene with Phoebe singing along to Ross playing the bagpipes will never fail to make me cry-snort with laughter.